NO FEAR

NO FEAR

In Business and In Life

Pilar Jericó

Managing Partner, InnoPersonas
Consulting

First published 2009 by
PALGRAVE MACMILLAN

Palgrave Macmillan in the UK is an imprint of Macmillan Publishers Limited,
registered in England, company number 785998, of Houndmills, Basingstoke,
Hampshire RG21 6XS.

Palgrave Macmillan in the US is a division of St Martin's Press LLC,
175 Fifth Avenue, New York, NY 10010.

Palgrave Macmillan is the global academic imprint of the above companies
and has companies and representatives throughout the world.

Palgrave® and Macmillan® are registered trademarks in the United States,
the United Kingdom, Europe and other countries.

ISBN-13: 978–0–230–58038–1
ISBN-10: 0–230–58038–6

This book is printed on paper suitable for recycling and made from fully
managed and sustained forest sources. Logging, pulping and manufacturing
processes are expected to conform to the environmental regulations of the
country of origin.

A catalogue record for this book is available from the British Library.

A catalog record for this book is available from the Library of Congress.

10 9 8 7 6 5 4 3 2 1
18 17 16 15 14 13 12 11 10 09

Printed and bound in Great Britain by
CPI Antony Rowe, Chippenham and Eastbourne

To Maribel and Pilar

CONTENTS

ACKNOWLEDGMENTS

Writing a book is like making a journey. I embarked on the adventure of NoFear in 1998, when I began to explore fear as a major handicap for companies and for people. I found, however, that libraries and universities did not have the sort of material I was looking for. Thus this journey had an additional difficulty which made it even more appealing. Along the way I drew on my experiences as a consultant and coach and on several months of interviews. NoFear has had four main accomplices: Pedro Luis Uriarte, Tomás Pereda, Luis Carlos Collazos, and Pilar Gómez Acebo. Thanks for your inspiration. And thanks to all of you with whom I had the chance to converse (Adriana Gómez-Arnau, Alberto García, Ángel Córdoba, Asunción Riera, Carlos Esteban, Carolina Maliqueo, Eduardo Bueno, Ignacio Bernabeu, Isabel Carrasco, Jaime Bonache, Jaime Pereira, Javier Fernández Aguado, Javier Quintana de Uña, José Cabrera, José María Gasalla, Luis Massa, Marcos Cajina, Techu Arranz, and friends from CESEDEN), to many other professionals from client companies, to my associates, to colleagues from the Department of Business Organization, to students from the School of

Business, and to alumni of the University, from whom I always learn.

I am grateful to Stephen Rutt, Eleanor Davey Corrigan, Vidhya Jayaprakash, Sandra Bruna, Natalia Berenguer, and Philip Wood for the love and energy they have put into this project.

And, of course, thanks to my family and my friends for their unconditional support (especially to Fran, Ana, Marta, Juan, Elena, Marisa, and Mariano), and to you, Álvaro.

INTRODUCTION

Fasten your seatbelts. We are about to enter the tunnel of fear. We all have fears. Every single one of us. However, the very mention of fear is taboo in companies. Only upbeat messages are allowed in business talks and advertising campaigns: Tommy Hilfiger-style models grinning on picture-perfect golf courses, websites about the delights of people management, and images of folks just thrilled to be mortgaging their lives for the next thirty years. And behind the scenes lies the hard reality: pressure to meet targets, power struggles, the risk of getting the sack, and, of course, our friend fear.

A brief point: If the term fear causes you certain "intellectual rash" or you simply prefer to ignore its existence, perhaps you would prefer to think of worry, anxiety, or stress. They all have something in common: they are emotions that kick in when we perceive threats and which take a heavy toll on our performance at work and on our lives in general. And although it is rarely acknowledged openly, fear has been employed as a management tool in business for centuries – and still is. Well, it's time to lift the gag order!

It's time to wake up to the heavy toll on our companies and on our lives! Only then will we see that there is another way – more difficult perhaps, but undoubtedly much more profitable – based on talent, change, and innovation. We are not talking about lab studies with rats, but systems that have been shown to work. There are companies and professionals who have taken the NoFear way with great success. We are not just talking about pretty words but about numbers, and happiness. Don't you think it's worth a try?

If we choose this course, we face challenges at two levels: in ourselves and in our companies. First: free ourselves from the horrible bind of fear. You may wear the best Dior suits and Hermes ties, but your insecurities will still straitjacket your potential. Second challenge: avoid fear-based management. Yes, we all know: it is the tried-and-true model of management and it works, or at least it has worked in the past. But horse-drawn carriages and matrix printers worked too. Past success is no guarantee of future success. Whether we are talking about a company or a person, the future is for those who are willing to make it; it is for those with the audacity to break the rules and grow upon their own strengths.

The challenge is NoFear. Do you dare accept?

> The brave man is not he who does not feel afraid, but he who conquers that fear.
>
> NELSON MANDELA

1

FEAR UNDER THE MICROSCOPE

CHILD OF MYTHOLOGICAL INFIDELITY

Fear is the child of a mythological act of infidelity. Venus, goddess of love, was not what we would call the perfect wife to her husband Vulcan, the god of fire, who was hardly pleased with her dallying about. Her most renowned affair was with Mars, the god of war, to whom she bore no fewer than five children: Cupid, Anteros, Harmony, Phobos, and Deimos. Cupid was the god of erotic love. Anteros, the god of requited love (less well known than his brother because, unfortunately, his touch is less frequent). Harmony personified unity. And, lastly, the sons who accompanied their father into battle: Phobos, whose name means "fear," and thus the term phobia; and Deimos, who stood for dread.[1] So, according to mythology, which sought to provide an explanation for human needs, fear descends from the union between Love and War.

Although the origin of the term fear has its roots in mythological events, in our language the word comes from the Old English *fær*. The New Oxford Dictionary of English defines fear as *an unpleasant emotion caused by the belief that someone or something is dangerous, likely to cause pain, or a threat.*[2] The threat may be physical (try provoking the boxer Mike Tyson) or mental (fear of losing my job). In the business world, mental threats, less intense but more constant over time, are the most common (although in certain sectors, such as construction, the circus or police forces, they are all too familiar with the former).

Fear is not an only child. In reality, it is a family of emotions that range from dread at having to speak in public to the stress caused by an announcement of downsizing (see Table 1.1). Some are material for couch therapy (phobias), others are linked to clearly defined, intense moments (panic). We will focus on the low intensity fears (Figure 1.1), since they are the ones that are responsible for undermining companies' performance and the ones with which we have the most room for maneuver.

Table 1.1   Some of fear's cousins

Term	Definition
Anxiety	Irrational fear not justified by external or internal causes
Stress	Type of anxiety linked to an external agent which provokes it (e.g., an overloaded schedule)
Fright	Momentary fear caused by a sudden stimulus (e.g., an unexpected explosion)
Phobia	Fear that goes far beyond reasonable caution in the face of danger (e.g., fear of spiders – tarantulas and other poisonous species apart)
Panic	Sudden appearance of intense fear associated with the urge to flee (e.g., a fire)

Source: Marks, I., *Fears, Phobias and Rituals*, London: Oxford University Press, 1987.

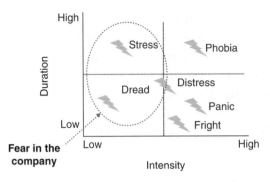

Figure 1.1 Locating fear in the business
Source: The author.

FEAR: NATURE OR NURTURE?

To Each Culture, Its Fear

Manhattan, early twentieth century. The first skyscrapers were being planned for the heart of New York. Problem: who would actually build them? Given that the tallest buildings at the time were only six or seven storey high, we can imagine the fears of workers at the thought of climbing up scaffolding a hundred meters high. But the skyscrapers were built, not because of the developers' powers of persuasion. Rather they came up with a creative solution: they hired Cherokee Indians who were used to heights and did not suffer vertigo. In addition to building the first skyscrapers, the Cherokees provided us with another key: fear is often culture-bound.

Each culture and each person can be characterized by a type of fear that varies over time and with the level of knowledge. While eclipses terrified primitive peoples, who interpreted them as messages from the gods, today we fret about how to anticipate and deal with natural disasters (or at least try to do so, as in the case of Hurricane Katrina). Fear has its roots in our biological makeup, but the more we know

3

about nature, for example, the fewer our uncertainties. Thus knowledge can serve to diminish our fears. However, in the business world uncertainty is part and parcel of the everyday scheme of things, creating fears more subtle than those derived from the threat of physical injury or death.

> Ignorance is the mother of fear.
> Henry Home Kames, philosopher (1696–1782)

Solid Ground, Please

Do you have vertigo? If so, you have a good excuse: fear of heights is written into our genes. This was shown in an experiment called *visual cliff*.[3] Two surfaces are joined: one opaque and the other transparent such that the latter seems to be suspended in midair. A baby several months old is placed between the two surfaces. In which direction does it crawl? In every case toward the opaque surface, as do other animals: chicks, cats, or monkeys (all except amphibians – ducks and turtles head right for the transparent surface).

We are born with fear of heights, independently of whether we suffer vertigo or have had a frightening experience. However, culture, education, and positive reinforcement can diminish our innate fears. This was seen in a variation on the above experiment in which 74 percent of the babies managed to cross the transparent surface when their mother was smiling at them from the other side![4] Good news for overcoming fears. Trust takes us to new heights; the absence thereof drowns us in fears.

> Treat a man as he is and he will remain as he is. Treat a man as he can and should be, and he will become as he can and should be.
> Goethe, poet (1749–1832)

Once the first skyscrapers had been built, a new challenge appeared: fear took hold of the users, who felt uneasy about the seemingly endless rides in the lifts. Once again, the solution was creative, using one of the most powerful tools for alleviating this type of anxiety: music. It was then that piped music – conceived to soothe people's nerves and help them to adjust to this new way of life – emerged. Today, with the exception of phobics, people do not often have reservations about taking lifts or working on the upper floors of skyscrapers (to which, curiously, many executives aspire). We have ridden lifts hundreds of times and learned that we are none the worse for it, although 9/11 awoke us to the existence of other sorts of dangers in skyscrapers.

In short, some fears we are born with, others we develop over the course of our lives, but we can overcome many. To eliminate the impact of fear is the challenge for NoFear companies and professionals.

The Brain's Short-Circuits[5]

Santiago Ramón y Cajal won the 1906 Nobel Prize for Medicine for his work on the human brain and many of his findings remain valid today. But he was wrong in one regard: as we age, our neurons do not die; rather the connections between them disappear. That is the conclusion of recent research by Michela Gallagher of Johns Hopkins University.[6] The neuronal connections, or synapses, keep us lively and young (perhaps developing and using our talents is like rubbing our brains with antiaging cream). When we experience pleasant situations, such as being among friends or working on a team we feel comfortable with, our neuronal connections are more fluid. Haven't you felt that you are often sharper in such situations? But the spark goes out when we feel fear. Fear can block or retard the electrical pulses between our neurons. Fear makes us less creative. And it makes us age more quickly: a poor recipe for longevity.

But there are more findings.[7] The thalamus is the control tower of our body, where all the data we receive from our surroundings is collected. From there it is sent to two brain systems:[8] the amygdala, where our feelings are located, and the neocortex, the seat of reasoning. And, curiously, the information goes first not to the neocortex, but to the amygdala.[9] In other words, we feel before we think. What does that mean? If in your workplace you experience threats or feel uncomfortable with your team, the amygdala will cast its net and enmesh your talent, and you will not be able to reason as clearly as you do in friendly environments. And, what's worse, you won't forget it easily. Another function of the amygdala is to act as your emotional memory. Which is why, though we may recall absolutely nothing of a meeting that bored us stiff, we remember perfectly which boss we do not want to work under.

> No passion so effectually robs the mind of all its powers of acting and reasoning as fear.
>
> Edmund Burke, politician and
> philosopher (1729–1797)

An Aged Brain

> We too often confront postmodern dilemmas with an emotional repertoire tailored to the urgencies of the Pleistocene.
>
> Daniel Goleman, author of
> *Emotional Intelligence*

Picture yourself driving along a highway (a real one, not the one from the BMW advert). Coming out of a tight curve you see a car bearing down on you in your lane. Danger, risk of accident. The thalamus has identified the information and will send it out along two circuits:[10] one short, which leads to the amygdala, and one long, to the neocortex. In milliseconds the amygdala will assume the reins of the emergency operation. From there, it will begin to send orders to the rest of the body.

The heart will be one of the first to receive orders and will start pumping faster to transport more oxygen. Blood circulation will be reorganized: to speed thinking and facilitate movement, the blood will be redirected from the skin and viscera to the brain and the muscles. Which is why you turn pale and need no artificial performance-enhancers to run like Ben Johnson. The pupils dilate to improve vision, and the coagulability of the blood increases in anticipation of possible injury. Certain glands come into play: those located at the lower part of brain and the suprarenals (above the kidneys) which produce adrenaline and noradrenaline. These are the stress hormones, responsible for stimulating the senses, and the source of the pleasure many derive from horror films and roller coasters. This hormonal dance will go on for seconds before you are aware that you have felt fear. And all that thanks to our biological evolution.

> We live as in the past, like we did 50,000 years ago, dominated by passions and base impulses. We are controlled by the emotional component, not by the cognitive component.
>
> Rita Levi-Montalcini, Nobel Prize winner
> for Medicine, 1986

The Zebras' Advice

> We build with our guts, not our brain.
>
> Pilar Gómez Acebo, president of the
> Spanish Federation of Women
> Executives and Entrepreneurs

We are different from zebras; there is no doubt about that, not only in the obvious ways, but also in other subtler ways: zebras do not suffer stress, according to Robert Sapolsky, a professor from Stanford University.[11] Zebras become terrified when they see a predator within range, and powerful hormonal reactions make them flee (faster than other zebras, rather than the predator, interestingly). But until they become aware of a hostile presence, they will graze peacefully without a thought for what they would do if a lion were to appear.

That's where we are different! Of all our emotions, fear is perhaps the one that has had the greatest impact on our evolution. We are paying a high price because of it. We've lived too long in caves and not long enough in cities! Fear kicks in without the need for any imminent risk to our physical integrity. It's enough to imagine that we are not going to meet our sales targets or that we cannot keep up with the mortgage payments – in short, whenever we conjure up distressing situations. And we are wonderful at imagining things. Our imagination, which at times is quite handy for making plans, only serves to set off the hormonal dance of fear at other times and lead us down the exhausting road of stress.

Stress and Cancer, Bosom Buddies

> When man leaves this world, nature will still be there.
>
> Hans Selye, doctor and pioneer
> of stress research (1907–1982)

Do you suffer stress at your job? If you do, join the crowd. You belong to the 10 percent of the world adult population with the same problem, according to a report from the International Labour Organization (ILO).[12] Of course, the rate is much higher in the industrialized countries. In the United States it is calculated that 43 percent of workers suffer stress[13] and that everyday one million people miss work due to its effects.[14] Stress looks bound to be the star illness of the twenty-first century.

When stress persists, corticoids come on the scene. They have earned well their name: *the hormones of fear*. In small amounts they are healthy. In continuous doses, however, they affect our immunological system, increasing the risk of cancer[15] and cardiovascular disease, while reducing our reproductive efficiency.[16] That is one of the reasons why some couples, who for years fail to have children, suddenly discover how fertile they are after they adopt children. Fertility and stress, a bad combination.

Apes Dressed in Fear

At a public debate in 1860 Samuel Wilberforce, the Bishop of Oxford, asked the biologist Thomas Henry Huxley, one of the prime defenders of theory of evolution:[17]

> Regarding your belief that you descend from an ape. Is it through your grandfather or your grandmother that you claim such descent?

We have *evolved* a great deal since then, even though just recently the states of Alabama and Oklahoma forced schools to put disclaimers on biology books stating that Darwin's theory was just one possibility.[18] Thanks to our evolution, we have a highly developed instinctive apparatus to manage our emotions. If you met a lion in the street, you wouldn't stop to wonder whether it was born in the wild or in the zoo. Fear will have you in flight before you know it. Our emotions are as old as the brains that control them, and they have helped us to get where we are as a dominant species (and to threaten others with extinction along the way).

> Emotions play a crucial role in our lives, they bring us together as people, they determine our quality of life and they are part of any relationship. They can save us or cause us real harm.
>
> Paul Ekman, professor, University of California, San Francisco

Do we all have fears? Yes, absolutely, as long as we have not suffered some sort of brain damage. Fear, sadness, and happiness are known as "basic" emotions.[19] In other words, all mammals share them, whether we are talking about a child in Guatemala, an executive in Tokyo, or a chimpanzee.[20] But they are not the only ones. Shame, shyness, contempt, and guilt are nonbasic or social emotions. They are transmitted culturally and are the reason why we sometimes feel like hiding under the table when it is someone else who makes a fool of oneself.

> All our knowledge has its origin in our perceptions.
>
> Leonardo da Vinci (1452–1519)

Let us stress something here: we are more intelligent thanks to our emotions (although Descartes and his Cartesian followers might find this claim heretical). Antonio Damasio, a professor of neurology at the University of Iowa, has shown that people with damage to the part of brain that stores emotions are unable to make decisions not based strictly on logic, such as choosing from among different types of bread for breakfast or the color of a suit.[21] All of our basic emotions have a reason for existing (Table 1.2). While fear is necessary to protect ourselves from threats, happiness enables us to repeat pleasurable activities. And our emotions are also inter-related, at least according to traditional Chinese medicine.[22] While the Chinese associate fear with water and locate it in the kidneys, they relate happiness to fire (located in the heart) and anger to wood (linked to the liver). An excess of water extinguishes fire or happiness, and produces an excess of wood, causing anger. A beautiful way of explaining emotional connections, and far from being an old wives' tale.

> We are sad because we cry.
>
> William James, philosopher and
> psychologist (1842–1910)

Table 1.2 Emotion, I need you

Emotion	What does it do for us?
Fear	Protects us from real or potential dangers
Happiness	Encourages us to repeat things that make us feel good
Surprise	Helps to orient us when faced with a new situation
Disgust	Makes us reject what we do not like
Anger	Leads us to destructive behaviour
Sadness	Facilitates the process of mourning, enabling us to accept loss

Note: Based on Ekman's studies and the identification of emotions in facial expressions. Nonetheless, it must be pointed out that there is no consensus on which emotions should be considered basic.

Source: Ekman, P. (1993): "Facial Expression of Emotion," *American Psychologist*, 48: 384–392.

DR. JEKYLL (TEMPERING FEAR), MR. HYDE (TOXIC FEAR)

We need fear! It helps to protect us from danger and it can also instil in us a sense of caution so that we do not speak our mind in front of the boss or quit our job before securing another one (although many play the lottery in the hope of having that luxury one day). Fear, therefore, *tempers* certain impulses that we have from a very early age. Parents play a critical role in its transmission. They teach their children not to lean too far out windows, not to play with electrical sockets, and to respect their teachers (although the last point is debatable). In short, we need tempering fear in order to be cautious. And as Aristotle would say, caution is the practical virtue of the wise.

However, this *tempering* (which restrains us from doing something foolish, we might add) is no longer positive when it paralyzes us and impedes us from using all of our potential. It is then that it becomes *toxic fear*. And toxic fear is most definitely both unnecessary and harmful to us and to the company. The prevalence of toxic fear has a high price in terms of the company's performance and our happiness. Unfortunately, however, it occurs quite commonly.

Tempering fear and toxic fear are intimately related. We might say that they are like the two sides of the same character in R. L. Stevenson's novel: Dr. Jekyll (tempering fear) and Mr. Hyde (toxic fear) (see Table 1.3). Both are born of the same emotion; in the novel, they are two aspects of the character of the doctor. Toxic fear is a distorted form of tempering fear. We all fear the rejection or loss of our loved ones (tempering fear), but it is a sign of toxic fear to mold

Table 1.3   Differences between Dr. Jekyll (tempering fear) and Mr. Hyde (toxic fear)

	Tempering fear	**Toxic fear**
Main qualities	Favorable to our interests. Has an evolutionary base.	Damaging to our interests. Does not aid our evolution.
Effects	Protects us from danger.	Stifles our talent. Hijacks our future.
Duration	Momentary.	Enduring.

Source: The author.

our everyday behavior in order to win the approval of those around us. And the consequences of the two types are very different, both in the novel and in real life.

> [Toxic] fear is an emotion that can reach high levels of intensity and that goes hand-in-hand with anxiety and distress, modifying substances in the organism and producing numerous psychosomatic phenomena.
>
> Ramiro Calle, author, *Los afectos*

What differences are there between tempering and toxic fear? The most important one is their effect. When tempering fear mutates into toxic fear, Mr. Hyde comes onto the scene to sap our strengths. It hijacks our future. It puts a brake on our talent, and on those of others, if we have leadership responsibilities. Tempering fear, on the other hand, is innocuous in terms of its effects on our performance. Another difference is duration. Toxic fear has an indefinite shelf-life (without any need for artificial preservatives); its impact on the decisions and behavior of sufferers, both on and off the job, is huge. Tempering fear, however, only makes its "cameo appearance" at certain moments. The difference is subtle, but not at all so the consequences of crossing the thin red line. And, unfortunately, when a business employs fear as a management tool, it throws the switch on our tempering fear and turns it into toxic fear (Mr. Hyde).

KEYS TO FEAR UNDER THE MICROSCOPE

- **All for one and one for all**: We all have fear. It is a basic emotion, one we share with all other mammals. It is activated when we perceive threats.

- **It is not an only child**: Fear encompasses a family of emotions that includes everything from stress, distress, and uneasiness to phobias, panic, and shock.

- **Nature or nurture?** We are born with innate fears, we develop others, and we can overcome a few thanks to positive reinforcement and experience.

- **It is not an invention**: Fear is a product of our evolution. It exists for a reason: it makes us smarter. It is housed in the limbic system of our brain.

- **I feel before I think**: Information from our surroundings is filtered by the limbic system first, then by the neocortex. If we feel fear, we are incapable of reasoning clearly.

- **Short-circuits**: Fear hamstrings our creativity and causes us to age more quickly. It produces short-circuits in the neuronal connections.

- **Hormonal dance**: Fear activates a hormonal dance in our body, generating adrenaline, noradrenaline (stress hormones), and corticoids (fear hormones), making us more susceptible to illness.

- **Dr. Jekyll (tempering fear), Mr. Hyde (toxic fear)**: Tempering fear is healthy; we need it. Toxic fear stifles employees' talents and hurts a company's profitability. The two fears are related, but their effects are quite different.

2

FEARS À LA CARTE

STAR WARS IN THE COMPANY

Two Sides of the Same Coin

Long, long ago, in a galaxy far, far away...

Thus begins one of the most successful sagas in the history of film: *Star Wars*. The first instalment came out in 1977 and for twenty years was the highest-earning film in the United States, until *Titanic* "sank" it to second.[1] *Star Wars* is a clear example of talent applied to cinema: the Hollywood-style marketing – undoubtedly the best – proved hugely effective and the director's choice of story was spot on. George Lucas wrote the screenplay in which the youthful Luke Skywalker faces the forces of evil led by the older Darth Vader (whose mask remains a top-seller at carnival time). But the basic plot of *Star Wars* was hardly new: rather it is a clever adaptation of the classic legend in which the hero must fight evil. And with this storyline it does not matter whether the characters live in the past, as with King Arthur and Merlin, or in the future, as with R2-D2 and his furry friend Chewbacca.

It is the thorns that make the rose.

Sufi proverb

Every hero needs his or her opposite in the form of an anti-hero, like Luke Skywalker and Darth Vader. The stronger and braver the hero, the more powerful the opponent. The same occurs in Eastern thought (yin and yang), in religion (heaven and hell), and in mythology (good and bad gods). And what is opposing force of fear? Motivation, without doubt. Fear and *motivation* are the two sides of the same coin. They arise from the same individual needs, they exist side by side, but they are quite different in character. *Motivation drives us to achieve a goal; fear mobilizes us to avoid a threat.* While motivation is sexy and CEOs love to talk about it, fear has been struck off from the lexicon of speeches. In the example of *Star Wars*, Darth Vader, dressed in black, personifies fear, while Luke Skywalker, in white of course, represents motivation. Both, however, are essential to understanding the behavior of employees in the workplace. And by focusing only on motivation we miss half the picture.

Do not underestimate the power of the force.

Star Wars, 1977

Five Fears for Five Reasons

Fear is my most loyal companion, it's never cheated on me.

Woody Allen, American actor,
film director and writer

But this companion has many faces. Each of us has one or more types of fear. And the same fear in two people can be perceived differently – further evidence of our complexity. Nevertheless, based on types of motivation, we can identify five main groups.

17

What motivates us at work? There's no easy answer. In fact, there are many theories which try to explain what it is, but perhaps one of the most widely accepted is by David McClelland.[2] According to McClelland, a Harvard professor, there are three types of motivation that inform our behavior at work: achievement, affiliation, and power or influence (Table 2.1). But these motivations are just one side of the coin. Lurking on the other side is our fear. Someone who is very achievement-oriented is likely to be terrified of failure. Someone who really needs to be included in the group will dread rejection or loneliness. For those motivated by influencing people, the loss of power can turn out to be their worst nightmare. Of

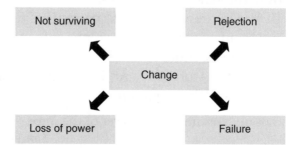

Figure 2.1 Main types of fear
Source: The author.

Table 2.1   What motivates us

What motivates us	Definition
Achievement	Reach a standard of excellence, overachieve.
Affiliation	Cultivate good relations with people
Power or influence	Influence others. Two types: *personalizing*, for individual benefit; *socializing*, for the benefit of the group

course, these are extreme cases. To these fears we should add two others of equal importance: the fear of not surviving (not making it to the end of the month) and the fear of change.

The five types of fear are closely related and one gives rise to many other fears (Table 2.2). All are tempering fears, to the extent that they help us to function on the job, but when they impact negatively on our talent, they become toxic fears. As we said above, Dr. Jekyll can turn into the terrible Mr. Hyde and take a toll on profits.

Table 2.2 For every motive, a fear

Main fear	Associated motivation	Some derivative fears
Failure to survive	Basic needs	■ Fear of losing one's job ■ The fear of not making it through the month...
Rejection	Feeling part of a group	■ Fear of being different ■ Fear of success or standing out ■ Fear of relating to people...
Failure	Achievement	■ Fear of error ■ Fear of assuming risks ■ Fear of making decisions ■ Fear of not being recognized for one's work...
Loss of power	Power – Influence	■ Fear of losing a position of influence ■ Fear of not being recognized socially...
Change	All of the above	■ Fear of a change in function ■ Fear of a change in location...

Source: The author.

Tell Me What Motivates You and I'll Tell You What Fears You Have

> The order of the universe is based on the complementarity of the opposing concepts.
>
> Ventura Ruperti and Jordi Nadal,
> authors of *Meditando el Management*

What is our most important fear? That of course depends on many factors: age, rank in the hierarchy, personal growth, etc. While an unqualified worker may worry about how to make it through the month, a business executive might be afraid of losing his rank and all that goes with it (the Audi, company Visa card, etc.). Nonetheless, certainly both the worker and the top executive have several fears that we talk about here. No one escapes fear, not even the Buddhist masters, one of whose favorite sayings is:[3]

> It is very rare that we do not have fear. Only when we panic.

If they say so, what about the ordinary people like us? But there is more: each of us harbors several fears at once. Our manual worker might be worried about not having influence over his or her colleagues and our executive about being rejected by his or her friends. However, if we had to choose a No. 1 fear in the company, the prize would go to fear of failure. At least that was what one study found from a sample of 185 mid-level managers and executives (Figure 2.2). And this makes sense: companies operate on the basis of objectives, and failing to meet them may involve unpleasant consequences.

However, even more interesting findings come out of the study. It was done in Spain. It is not surprising, then, that fear of rejection should be so important. Nor is it strange that loss of power should be the least named fear. Does it

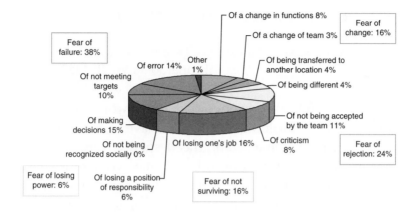

Figure 2.2 What am I afraid of?

Source: Talento Miedo y Resultados, study carried out between April and June 2005 with seminar and conference attendees in Spain. Total sample: 185 upper and middle managers.

not exist? Are Spaniards somehow immune to the temptations of power? In a society where feeling part of a group is very important, such as Spain, people are somewhat reluctant to say that they are motivated by telling others what to do. And, if in speaking about motivation, the seductive side of the coin, we hardly seem honest with ourselves, can we be sincere when talking about our fears?

The important thing is not just to know our own fears, but also to identify the fears we cause in others. Outstanding member of a highly competitive team? He or she can spark the fear of failure in the others or the fear of not surviving in someone who is insecure about their job. Attitudes such as withholding information, refusing to work on a given project or forming cliques can be explained in terms of our friend fear.

Drum roll, moment of truth. It is time to ask ourselves: What types of fears do we have and which ones do we cause?

FIRST FEAR: NOT MAKING IT THROUGH THE MONTH

> He who possesses most must be most afraid of loss.
> Leonardo da Vinci (1452–1519)

Have you ever felt like never going back to work? If you are made of flesh and blood, surely you have at some point. And if so and you have renounced such a venture, you probably thought of, among other things, your mortgage, the kids' school, or the payments on the car. The motives correspond to a more basic fear:[4] *the fear of not surviving* (or of not making it through the month, in everyday language). This fear arises from our instincts. Just as animals defend their food, we need to protect that which enables us to enjoy shelter and sustenance. That's why the incidence of ulcers and depression rockets in periods of economic crisis, when the job market is especially tight.

When the Mortgage Enters Your Life

If you do not wish to suffer the fear of not making it through the month, there are several alternatives (if not feasible, at least legal): enter the time tunnel, go back to the past and strike out marriage, mortgages and children, and shed all financial burdens; win the lottery, if you play; or...acquire a skill that is in demand. Of course, there are many other options that we have not mentioned: one of the more pragmatic ones is to limit your material ambitions so that you can satisfy them with any old job. That is the chosen lifestyle of some people from developed countries, who work six months out of the year and spend the rest of the year travelling from place to place, like David Carradine in the old series *Kung Fu*. Certainly that must seem a strange existence for us slaves to the clock.

Freedom from financial burdens is a considerable help in alleviating this fear. And countless young people all over the world aspire to just that. Only 19 percent of Spaniards between the ages of 18 and 29 move out of their parent's home.[5] We hardly need mention the social consequences involved.

Things change when we buy a home. But indebtedness is not the only reason for fear to grow. The stork, when it comes, brings more. With kids responsibilities multiply – by two, by three, or whatever the number. No longer is our fear only for ourselves; now it is for the family, too. And let's not even talk about divorce and having to support two households. It's like the old circus number: if you think that was a good trick... That's why people with family responsibilities and few chances of finding another job tend to be more cautious (or act less freely) when faced with certain decisions such as confronting management or supporting a union.

How do we recognize the fear of not making it through the month? Try consulting your pillow. When income does not cover expenses, nights feel longer than ever, and you find yourself over and over having the same conversation with trusted friends. And how do we spot this fear in the company? It all has to do with employability, or rather, the chance one has of getting another job, which depends on how marketable one's skills are at the time.

> Talent, not the company, chooses.
> Luis Carlos Collazos, former Director Human Resources,
> Hewlett Packard Spain

Free of Fear

> If 20 people left Microsoft, the company would risk bankruptcy.
> Bill Gates, cofounder of Microsoft

Not bad if you happen to be among Mr. Gates's twenty. But Microsoft employs over 50,000 people, and clearly not all of them enjoy the same power as the chosen few, nor the same salary, nor the same appeal on the job market. Having the right skills, which implies the freedom to switch jobs, diminishes the fear of not making it through the month. Those who know that other companies are on the look-out for people with their talent often have that extra bit of pride and pluck that makes them less sensitive to the threat of getting sacked. Therein lies, perhaps, one of the reasons such people may cause problems for management; they can question the status quo, something which clashes with the insecurities of certain managers or colleagues. But this sort of talent is rare, and people whose skills are in demand still do not escape other fears, as we shall see below.

Government employees are a case apart. If it was not for the job security, how many would chose to work for the government? The knowledge that one cannot be sacked acts as buffer against this type of fear. Of course, civil servants suffer other fears. The inflexibility of the system can make life difficult and the pay is hardly generous. Indeed, as a group, civil servants suffer one of the highest rates of chronic depression and associated sickness absence – although a cynic might say that, unfortunately for the rest of us, only civil servants can take such leave without the risk of finding a pink slip on their desk when they get back.

Thermometer of the Fear of Not Surviving

> If the Traditional work relationship, that is, for life, was like a marriage, the new relationship is like an endless succession of divorces and remarriages.
>
> Peter Capelli, author of the book
> *The New Deal at Work*

In the United States between 1980 and 1995 the estimated number of workers affected by downsizing ranges from a minimum of 13 million to the spectacular figure of 39 million.[6] Not bad for a work force of some 130 million. It is estimated that the number of companies that outsourced part of their production (with the attendant sackings) trebled between 1998 and 2000.[7] Market globalization, relocation of manufacturing, mergers, changes in management – all prime examples of what activates the fear of not surviving. Little wonder the traditional commitment to the company is on the way out, or that we spend more time engaged in jockeying for position in the company when we don't know what the future holds. If I perceive a risk of losing what I have, the fear of not surviving can act like a rope around my neck, the strands of which are the following:

- Vulnerability to losing current job
- Difficulty of finding another job
- Financial burden
- Level of training

If the rope is tight enough, fear can strangle you. It is then that the risk of sacking becomes the Sword of Damocles that falls on the new home, car, or the private school. And such fear is one of the causes of *knowledge-is-power*-type behavior. If I share what I know, I am no longer indispensable and they can sack me. Better to keep it to myself, although that may be bad for the company. To think and act in this way is human, but it is also the worst way to cultivate talent and, paradoxically, it works against our interests. The less we give, the less we receive. And the less we receive, the more vulnerable we are to becoming redundant and losing our job. In other words, instead of protecting us, this sort of attitude

Figure 2.3 Some of the strands of the fear of not surviving
Source: The author.

pushes us into the arms of fear. It is a terrible vicious circle that **NoFear** companies and people must break.

In sum, the fear of not making it through the month is fear associated with having or, rather, losing what one has. And what are *you* afraid of losing?

SECOND FEAR: I NEED TO BE LOVED!

> Man is a social animal by nature.
>
> Aristotle (384–322 AD)

Experiencing the Asch effect

Take a look at the two cards in Figure 2.4. Which line on card B is the same length as the line on card A? So long as your eyes are good enough, you'll probably pick number 3. And what if you were in a group and all the others picked

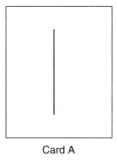 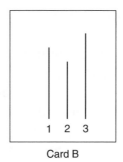

Card A   Card B

Figure 2.4 The Asch effect
Source: The author.

line 2, would you stick to your answer? Eighty percent of young people would change their opinion. That is what an experiment with American university students by the social psychologist Solomon Asch showed,[8] in which an unwitting student was asked to leave the room and the other students plotted with the professor to pick line 2 as the right answer: when the victim returned only one in five stood by their original answer. The experiment was done in Japan and Germany and the findings were equally scandalous. Reason: peer pressure, individual insecurities, and the underlying *fear of rejection*. By the way, the Asch effect, as it is called, also affects companies. It might not be quite as obvious as it is in Asch's original experiment, but how often have we changed our stance when everyone else insisted we were wrong? If it has ever happened to you, now you know: you've been a victim of the Asch effect.

> You and I are one and the same thing. I cannot hurt you without harming myself.
>
> Mahatma Gandhi
> (1869–1948)

A Bad Team for Vietnam

Smart people sometimes make dumb decisions. That would seem to be the case with U.S. President Lyndon Johnson and his advisors with regard to the Vietnam War. The failure of certain decisions in that war inspired Yale University professor Irving Janis to investigate what had happened. He called it *groupthink*.[9] It occurs in highly cohesive teams, more so if they share an ideal (or a 'mission from God', as some U.S. presidents must have thought). Groupthink happens when everyone thinks in the same way and there are no cracks through which alternative proposals might seep in. In other words, if they believed that they had to stay the course in Vietnam, no one said otherwise. It is not just that they could not say it: they were not even allowed to think it. The consequences of groupthink should provide food for thought: farewell to alternatives, farewell to the experts who believe otherwise, farewell to any other way of understanding the information. As Ridderstråle and Nordström might have put it, groupthink makes you live a *karaoke moment* as an echo of your favorite pop star instead of being yourself.

> The social impulse does not rest directly upon the love of society, but upon the fear of solitude.
> Arthur Schopenhauer, philosopher (1788–1860)

At the root of both the Asch effect and groupthink lies the fear of rejection. We all need to feel part of a group, whether we rally round friendship, a company, a football team, or a brand of beer. We need the *warmth of the stable*, as Nietzsche said. We harbor the conflicting urges to feel different and to identify with a group or *tribe*. And our fear of isolation has a biological basis. The human child is the most vulnerable in the entire animal kingdom. While a colt takes just a few hours to learn to walk, we need months of constant support and patience from our long-suffering parents. We are not prepared to stand on our own. What we lack genetically we make up for with culture. As the sociologist Cristobal Torres says: "A wolf raised among humans is still a wolf; a human raised among wolves behaves like a wolf."[10] And culture is acquired through interaction with others. Being alone is a not very gratifying experience for most people (hermits apart). The fear of rejection, therefore, has a tempering origin, and manifests itself directly in the company or at the football ground.

> Men cannot live if they lack forms of mutual cooperation.
> Erich Fromm,
> philosopher (1900–1980)

When Being the Chosen One Is a Disaster

> Man dreads to be alone.
> Honoré Balzac, writer (1799–1850)

Imagine a prestigious publishing house. They promote their top salesman to sales manager and he is now much less happy in his work. Not because he dislikes earning more money or having "manager" embossed on his card, but because he's no longer one of the *gang*. His old colleagues, the ones he always went out for a drink with at fairs, treat him differently. He's the boss now. He has to make demands on them, play the role of the *bad guy*, and maybe even, on orders from higher up, sack someone. In his longed-for years as a salesman, his strength was his way with people; an affiliative, empathetic person who succeeded in convincing his customers with the selling-points of the product. In short, a winning spirit who does not like being a boss – though he might find that out too late.

His main strength had become his main trouble. His affiliative motivation and his people-oriented nature concealed a more silent fear, the fear of rejection. And in a position of authority it now begins to show itself. This is a real case which ended as one might expect: a letter of resignation. And it is just one of many other stories that tells us why many middle managers fail at the job of supervising their former colleagues. "They stopped asking me to go for a coffee with them," a hospital administrator commented sadly. Often implicit in the fear of rejection is the fear of success or of being seen as different. Making this sort of person the *chosen one* is the worst favor you can do them (no matter how often they are unaware of the fact).

Latin Self, Affiliative Self

> Religion and nationalism, as well as any custom and any belief however absurd and degrading, if it only connects the individual with others, are refuges from what man most dreads: isolation.
>
> Erich Fromm, philosopher (1900–1980)

Following Fromm's reasoning, companies also act as refuges in the struggle against isolation. Working in a large corporation provides many people with a sense of belonging and, what's worse, it gives meaning to their lives. You are sure to know more than one such person. And who are the biggest slaves to the fear of rejection? Those who need to belong to a group. In other words, those with a more affiliative motivation or who seek in the group a haven from the isolation from which we all flee.

This is another important difference between the Latin world and the developed English-speaking countries (the Anglosphere): the former culture tends to seek harmony among people, while the latter is more focused on achievement. In other words, one of the greatest cultural fears among Latin people is social rejection. And this is evident in the stage fright many suffer when they have to speak in front of others. MIT professor Nicholas Negroponte once gave a lecture at a Madrid business school and when he asked for any questions, a deathly silence fell over the room. No one raised their hand. Had there been at least one brave soul, the rest might have followed. Negroponte left with that sinking sensation that one gets in such cases: either they understood everything perfectly, or they understood nothing at all.

This fear is also at the root of the dread of looking ridiculous, so acute in Latin cultures. Americans and the Japanese, on the other hand, are not at all shy about engaging in foolish games in front of the whole world or making a hash of a song in a karaoke club – and without a drop of alcohol to give them the courage. That would be unthinkable for many people from Latin countries, always sheltered behind their beloved wall of *false modesty* and so concerned with what people will say.

> I am myself and my circumstance, and if I do not save it, I do not save myself.
> José Ortega y Gasset, philosopher (1883–1955)

Such fears are much stronger among young people. The majority of first-year Spanish public university students in classrooms with over seventy peers hardly ever put questions to the professor. And it is not because they do not have any, but because of peer pressure. To stand out is frowned upon and someone who does so may bear the brunt of criticism from peers. This behavior is at the opposite end of the spectrum from that of other cultures. In the United States, for example, the professor shows up for the first day of class and following a brief presentation of the course, politely asks: "Any questions?" He will probably see 70 percent of the hands shoot up to ask all sorts of questions (albeit, some rather odd), without the slightest fear of what the others might think.

Why is belonging to a group so important in Latin countries? A study by David McClelland[11] came up with the key: religion. Catholicism stresses the affiliative spirit more than the drive to achieve, the classic attribute of Protestantism. Which is why Ireland, although English-speaking, is one of the most affiliative countries in the world, according to this study. Irish pubs, their music, and general merriment would seem to corroborate this.

THIRD FEAR: ALLERGIC TO FAILURE

> There is only one thing that makes a dream impossible to achieve: the fear of failure.
>
> Paulo Coelho, writer

A Stain-Remover for Failure

Your success in this world is a sign of what you will obtain in the hereafter is a Protestant maxim, quite different from the Catholic saying *the last will be the first*.[12] Once again religion underlies the Protestant drive to achieve. McClelland[13] embarked on the adventure of discovering what it is that makes the United States different from the rest of the world. And he found what he dubbed "achievement motivation" (to achieve more than others, of course). Years earlier philosophers such as Erich Fromm had come to the same conclusion. Lutheranism and Calvinism held work and efficiency as supreme values. No wonder that the bells of the Nuremberg Cathedral became the first to strike the quarter hours: in sixteenth-century Germany time was already of the essence![14] Result: hard work and achievement were the keys to the new Protestant culture, which, of course, capitalism inherited. It is hardly surprising that England was the cradle of capitalism.

> Success came to be the sign of divine grace; failure, that of condemnation.
>
> Erich Fromm, philosopher (1900–1980)

Companies provide an extraordinary breeding ground for a common affliction: the fear of failure. How many of us have been sacked and then hid the fact? And not only in job interviews, where we all put on the mask of the *super-professional-never-been-sacked-from-any-company*, but in less tense settings too. And it is not because we have converted to Protestantism (please, let us not offend the Vatican), but because we have learned to interpret failure as a stain. Either we remove it with some justification – "I was going to quit but they beat me to it" – or we pretend it did not happen – "No, no, I wasn't sacked, I quit."

Slaves to Success

At the age of eighteen years Alexander the Great took command of his father's army. He had had the benefit of one of greatest teachers in history, Aristotle. Alexander had a keen mind and his ambition knew no bounds. However, historians stress another essential quality for understanding his achievements: the desire to outdo his father (of course, the Spartan education he received from his tutor and his mother helped, too). And if there is anything we can be sure of it is that Alexander was no Protestant. He was born eighteen centuries before Luther nailed his Ninety-Five Theses to the door of the Wittemberg castle church. Still, his focus on achievement was what drove him. But Alexander is not alone. Mozart and Oedipus were also motivated by the same desire to outdo their fathers. Sometimes it is more subtle: *I wanted to be number one because I thought that it would make my father love me more.* A very intimate desire with which many people can identify. And if you are like that, dear friend, you are a member of the exclusive club of the slaves to success. And hats off to the company that hires you!

However, to be motivated by achievement you needn't be a Protestant or have had a traumatic relationship with your father. It can derive from your education or even, according to McClelland,[15] interaction between siblings.

I Pass If You Fail

> Failure-tolerant leaders break down the barriers that separate them from their followers and they engage at a personal level with the people they lead.
>
> Richard Farson and Ralph Keyes,
> authors of *The Paradox of Innovation*

In 2004, Amena, a telecommunications firm, did a ranking of their employees by team. Each team leader was asked to rate their workers from best to worst. For those at the bottom, needless to say, the writing was on the wall. Arthur Andersen, the auditor that went bust following the Enron scandal, did the same, ranking their best and worst employees and dispensing with those who came in last. This sort of technique reinforces overachievement-oriented behavior. Not only do you have to do it right, but you have to do it better than your colleagues (or rivals?). Some of us might find this practice rather "aggressive," but this spirit drives Americans from the earliest years of their childhood. And, like it or not, a good deal of the techniques we apply in the companies are borrowed from the big corporations (performance ratings, leadership development) or used on the advice of Anglosphere consultants or gurus.

In many American schools and universities a passing grade is only awarded to those who perform above the peer average. In other words, if the others have done extraordinarily well on the exam and I've done just so-so, I fail (and if the others scrape by and I do a bit better, I'm on the honor role). In other words, I pit myself not only against a battery of tough questions, but also against my entire group of peers. What better way to instil the drive to achieve?

If you didn't receive enough achievement motivation in your upbringing, don't worry. The company will take care of "helping" you to develop it. As we said above, today the competition is so fierce that achievement motivation is far more than just a fad; it is a vital necessity, and workers are under ever greater pressure to produce results and beat the clock doing it.

From a Bold Decision to the Renaissance

Florence, 1417. Of all the city's buildings, the Orsanmichele was perhaps the best reflection of its society. Wheat was stored on the upper floor, the lower floor was reserved for administrative tasks, and the exterior for marketing in the style of the day: the city's guilds showed off their power in sculptures occupying niches in the building's façades. Besides the obvious references to the guild's trade, this early form of advertising included another standard feature: a representation of the guild's patron saint. The wealthier the guild the bigger and better the niche. The most coveted were on the part of the façade overlooking the Palazzo della Signoria, city hall, and large enough to accommodate the saint and attendant figures. Meanwhile, the poorest guild, the armorers – whose trade was by then decline in Florence where the old warrior class had abandoned its arms in favor of commerce – had to make do with the worst niche: on a corner and shallower than the others, being as it was that the stairway to the upper floor was located just behind it. The armorers' patron saint was George, the knight who slays the dragon to save the princess, and in that niche only a cramped, kneeling St George fit. Not exactly a dignified pose for a knight, but, of course, then as now, money talks.

The armorers' guild sought out Donatello and charged him with the difficult task of coming up with a dignified St. George. And he broke the rules laid down in the canons of the period. He came up with a St George who stood strong and powerful, the only problem being that it did not fit in the tight space of the niche. The solution was worthy of a genius: he brought the body out of the niche to stand out beyond the plane of the façade. His decision, bold as it was, marked the beginning of the Renaissance in sculpture.

> Problems are only opportunities in work clothes.
>
> Sun Tzu, general and author
> of *The Art of War* (500 AD)

Sun Tzu states that any problem holds out an opportunity, but this implies risk. Donatello followed this maxim, just as innovative companies do. But the fear of failure collides head-on with this attitude. If Donatello had played by the rules, the Renaissance would not have arisen from his hands. Questioning the rules is the first step toward innovation. Trailblazing companies know that rarely is the cry of *eureka!* heard on the first attempt. For each success story, there are ten of trial and error. If you punish mistakes, you cut your chances of greater success in the future. And you reinforce people's natural tendency to associate mistakes with guilt or the *I'm-no-good* feeling. Taking bold decisions entails assuming the price of error. When achievement becomes an obsession, that price will look very prohibitive. And, worse still, when, as with Alexander the Great, the pursuit of success is the driving force in our lives, failure kicks the legs out from under our self-esteem.

> The art of winning is learned in defeat.
>
> Simón Bolivar,
> soldier and politician (1783–1830)

Another derivative of the fear of error and failure is perfectionism. The perfectionist wants to control everything down to the last detail, so that no one, starting with the perfectionist, can say that something is not right. In these situations, the demands come from within the self, or rather from *self-punishment*. As soon as the perfectionist thinks he or she has done something wrong, the mental torture begins. A perfectionist does not need to be controlled. They demand it of themselves. But they pose two problems: first, the extent to which they suffer for their "masterpiece;" second, the risk of their work and that of others becoming paralyzed. Rather than risk failure, the perfectionist prefers to do nothing, to the loss of potential long-term benefits.

The Approval-Seekers

> As much as we thirst for approval we dread condemnation.
> Hans Selye, doctor and father
> of stress research (1907–1982)

Do you feel appreciated in your work? Lack of approval is a great motivation-killer. We need approval; it is a necessary part of our development.[16] We need it first from our parents, then from the people who matter to us most. A successful executive once said that when he first embarked on his career he sought the approval of those above him. This led him to positions of greater responsibility and to greater achievements. But once he had reached a point of personal satisfaction, it was the approval of his peers that began to matter most. Just like growing up, perhaps.

However, when someone has an overriding need for approval, the problem emerges once again, in the form of an inability to act without positive feedback. At the root of this lies a chilling fear of failure.

> Every battle is won before it is fought.
> Sun Tzu, general and author
> of *The Art of War* (500 AD)

It is interesting because when we desperately seek approval from someone (of course, hardly anyone openly admits doing so), we give that person power over us. Think of someone highly motivated by social success and who is always looking for approval for everything they do. This person may be extremely vulnerable to criticism. Any comment which might cast doubt on their work can feel like a ton of bricks. Logically, we tend to seek the approval of those whom we admire; but we also want it from those who wield control over our success. But if you know a real approval-seeker you will notice that they may also be susceptible to comments from people who do not belong to either of those groups. And the reason is simple: the approval-seeker has given them that power. At its root, their focus on achievement is grounded in insecurity, which makes such people extremely vulnerable.

And now think of yourself: to whom do you award such power in your life?

FOURTH FEAR: CLINGING TO POWER

> Fame is one means to silence one's doubts. It has a function to be compared with that of the Egyptian pyramids or the Christian faith in immortality.
>
> Erich Fromm, philosopher (1900–1980)

The Forbidden Motivation

What most motivates people in their work – career, money, a balanced personal and professional life? Well, it depends. For each person the motivation is different, and not only that but it changes over time. We do not know if it is because you mature (a nice way of saying "get old"), you move on from one stage to another or you simply shift into a new role. But the upshot is that motivation changes, which complicates considerably the job of managing people in a company. And there is another difficulty: we are not always aware ourselves of what we want.

> It is hard to know what we like. Most people fool themselves in this regard. It is rare to know oneself well.
>
> Robert Henri, painter (1865–1929)

A clear example of this is the findings from surveys done in several countries with executives interested in talent-based management (Table 2.3). The question was simple: how

Table 2.3   What motivates executives

ARGENTINA	CHILE
1. Furthering of career	1. Continuous development
2. Continuous development	2. Furthering of career
3. Sharing a mission	3. A good work–life balance
4. A good work–life balance	4. Sharing a mission
5. Using advanced technologies	5. Working with people one likes
6. Working with people one likes	6. High pay
7. High pay	7. Using advanced technologies
8. Working with a prestigious organization	8. Working with a prestigious organization
9. Job security	9. Social recognition
10. Social recognition	10. Job security
SPAIN	**COLOMBIA**
1. Continuous development	1. Continuous development
2. Sharing a mission	2. Balanced personal-professional life
3. Furthering of career	3. Furthering of career
4. A good work–life balance	4. Sharing a mission
5. Working with people one likes	5. Using advanced technologies
6. High pay	6. Social recognition
7. Working with a prestigious organization	7. Working with a prestigious organization
8. Using advanced technologies	8. Working with people one likes
9. Social recognition	9. High pay
10. Job security	10. Job security

Table 2.3   Continued

GUATEMALA	MEXICO[a]
1. Continuous development	1. Continuous development
2. Furthering of career	2. Job security
3. Sharing a mission	3. Working with a prestigious organization
4. A good work–life balance	4. High pay
5. Working with a prestigious organization	5. Working with people one likes
6. High pay	6. Furthering of career
7. Job security	7. Social recognition
8. Using advanced technologies	8. Using advanced technologies
9. Working with people one likes	9. A good work–life balance
10. Social recognition	10. Sharing a mission

Note: [a] The method and sample used in the Mexican study was different from that used in other countries, with individual interviews with small and medium companies. I am grateful to Magda Evelia Mendoza and the people from the Universidad Autónoma de Sinaloa for their kind support.

Source: Results of surveys down on attendees at talent management congresses in Buenos Aires (Argentina, 2001), Madrid and Barcelona (Spain, 2001), Bogotá (Colombia, 2001), Santiago (Chile, 2001), and Guatemala City (Guatemala, 2003). The sample was 800 mostly upper and middle managers from large and medium companies. In the case of Mexico, the survey was done in Culiacán (Mexico, 2005) in individual interviews with mostly small companies, with the collaboration of Magda Evelia Mendoza and the team from the Universidad Autónoma de Sinaloa.

motivating are the following factors for you? As the data show, there are some differences between countries, but overall the top choices were: furthering of career, continuous development, sharing a mission, and a balanced personal and professional life. But perhaps the most intriguing findings are which factors come last: job security and social approval. Let's have a look.

The first surveys were done in 2001. That was the year in which the financial bubble started to POP, and as in the past, widespread lay-offs were the preferred solution to the crisis. Nonetheless, despite the uncertainty of the period, the executives said that job security was not what most motivated them. And to an extent they were right. Herzberg[17] coined the term "hygiene factors" for those factors which do not appear to be very motivating so long as they exist, but when absent are highly demotivating. Thus, both job security and approval may be merely hygienic questions for most executives. But if they did not exist, would they merit so little consideration? Judging by the mass flight of talent from Internet companies to more established companies with greater prestige it would seem that they would not. This is also seen in the preference for working for a well-known company rather than for one whose mission remains largely a mystery, no matter how solid, multinational, and wonderful it might be (over time this changes). But what is worse, although we seek prestige, which is a form of power, we do not like to admit it openly, as seen in surveys and outplacement interviews.

When executives lose their job, one of their first concerns is their family and the drop in the standard of living for them, according to Pilar Gómez Acebo, based on her more than fifteen years of experience in outplacement. However, when the outplacer offers a similar job with better pay, but in a less prestigious company, many say no:

"Why aren't you interested in the job? Aren't you concerned about your children's schooling?" "Yes, but what about my prestige?"

Indeed, the fear of loss of power (loss of prestige, in this case) comes into play, although few want to admit it. In the Anglosphere people are less circumspect. Tom Peters claims that the first thing we defend is our own name. He says that each of us is the head of our own business – Me, inc. – and that our primary job is to sell our own brand.[18] Clearly Tom Peters speaks from his own experience; he is an expert on the subject. Robert Greene states in one of his forty-eight laws of power that: "Almost everything depends on your prestige; defend it with your life."[19] And the hungriest of all power-seekers, politicians, spend vast amount of money on image advisers. There must be some reason.

Admit it: it's not only top-level executives who are vulnerable to the fear of loss of power, we all are. Power casts its spell over all sorts of people: middle managers, union leaders, presidents of associations, teachers, preachers, and media stars – all of whom share a strong need to influence people. Perhaps power is the siren song we want to hear, although we think of ourselves as Ulysses bound to the mast. Our values once again?

> One of the most important features of society is the use of power.
>
> Thomas Hobbes, philosopher (1588–1679)

Glued to the Seat of Power

> But to Be a leader means, especially, having the opportunity to make a meaningful difference in the lives of those who permit leaders to lead.
>
> Max De Pree, writer on leadership

Lucciano Benetton and Richard Branson both have charisma and empathy. They influenced people before they founded their companies, without the need for any position of power. Later, when they set up Benetton and Virgin, respectively, they added the power they derived from a feat of this magnitude to their natural leadership abilities. They are, of course, two rather exceptional people.

The fear of loss of power appears in people who are motivated to influence others through either *legitimate power* (legitimate in the sense that it derives from the hierarchy) or charismatic power,[20] also known as leadership. Let's look at an example. First case: Joaquín, a not so brilliant engineer who has risen to middle management in strict accordance with the Peter Principle: *In any hierarchy people tend to rise to their own level of incompetence.*[21] The other candidates for this job moved to other companies and he was the only one left. His *loyalty* to the company and his seniority (he never had many offers from other companies) led management to pick him to lead a team. And he was delighted. He had been hoping for such a promotion for a long time, because one of the basic aspects of his motivation was his need to influence others. Second case: Antonio, also an engineer; highly talented, although technically speaking not the best on the team. He is an informal leader. His way of speaking, his energy, and his ability make him the center of attention. He succeeds in getting his colleagues involved. He loves to have people listen to him and pay attention to what he says. Influence motivates him too, but a far cry from how it motivates Joaquín. If you had to choose a type of power, which would you prefer, Joaquín's or Antonio's?

The difference in power depends on who is influenced. So-called legitimate power is obtained from the hierarchy, as in the case of Joaquín. Management puts someone in a position of power and those now under him or her, in this case former peers, have to put up and shut up. On the other hand, with charismatic power the only source of influence is those willing to give it. No one forces Antonio's colleagues or friends to pay attention to what he says. They do so because they want to. Hierarchical power only exists thanks to management's "divine intervention"; charismatic power is grounded in personal qualities. Leaders have followers. The hierarchical boss on the other hand will always have subordinates. This difference can be largely put down to fear. Those who cling hardest to power are the ones least sure of being able to regain their position by their own means. Their insecurity is like Superglue on their seat of power.

The Sexiness of Power

> I was the son of immigrants and with by working hard, I managed, little by little, to rise to be president of Ford. Once I got the job, I felt like I was on the roof of the world. But fate told me: "Wait, we haven't finished with you yet, now you're going to find out what it's like to be dropkicked off Mount Everest!"
>
> Lee Iacocca, former president of Ford and former chairman of Chrysler

Indeed, wielding power has that risk and that sexiness. As the former U.S. Secretary of State Henry Kissinger said when asked how a man of his modest looks always managed to have a beautiful woman on his arm: "Power is the ultimate aphrodisiac." It is true, power attracts. Public figures are sexier than nobodies. And, for a great many people, a manager or a chairman is sexier than a technician; partly because they have the approval of the organization, and partly because he or she is the boss and, sometimes, a leader.

Power is a drug. And it is a tough habit to kick. "Influencing the lives of others is a way of overcoming your own doubts," said Fromm. When the people are forced to do what you say and you are in a position to mete out reward or punishment, power acts as a balm for your own insecurities. In some positions of power, the person stands alone for the company[22] and all eyes are on him or her. "The burden of responsibility is very heavy," says one executive director. "You can't have a bad day. When I went to present company growth charts to a meeting of analysts, I had to put on a happy face even when I'd slept badly the night before for entirely different reasons. People associate your behaviour and appearance with how well the company is doing..."

In certain situations, managers will create a public face for themselves, which they put on in order to deal with their responsibilities, dismissing people if necessary, and it is the only personality their fellow workers ever see. A mask that many managers (and not just at the top), politicians, and celebrities end up wearing. What are the advantages of separating the public personality from the private one? It creates a shield against "mundane problems" and makes exercising power relatively painless. And the disadvantage? The personal cost is high, because you can end up believing you are that public personality, as happened to the actor Johnny Weissmuller, who played Tarzan so many times he ended up in a mental hospital and died there in 1984 still believing he was the King of the Jungle.

When Someone Acts like a Baboon

Life is good at the top, as baboon chiefs know. Stanford professor Robert Sapolsky[23] has studied stress in mammals and observed that when the dominant male gets stressed he vents his anger on those directly below him, who then pass it on down to the next level, and so on until there is no one left to get angry with. Sounds familiar? The same tendency to pass threats all the way down the hierarchy exists in companies. It starts somewhere and snowballs its way down through the ranks, unless there is someone along the way who is capable of absorbing the "blows" without passing them on. And there is no doubt that that very quality – being able to overcome the biological instinct to behave like a baboon – is one of the key points to being a good boss.

> An executive has to be a retaining wall against threats being passed on down. When he does that, the productivity of his team rises considerably.
>
> Tomás Pereda, *human resources director, Hertz Spain*

However, there is yet another factor that reinforces the fear of loss of power: personal risk. Certain positions demand a high degree of personal commitment. In the event of a merger or a change in management, the heads most likely to roll are the ones near the top. When the IT specialist is in charge of a project which goes wrong, he has other companies to try his luck with. The executive market, however, is a bit tighter. And as if that were not enough, the higher up you sit the more visible you are. When the boss is in trouble he cannot hide; he is on public trial.

FIFTH FEAR: NO CHANGES, PLEASE

The Chess Game of Change

As Ridderstråle and Nordström say:[24]

> When the top golfer in the world is black;
> the most popular rap singer is white;
> France accuses the United States of arrogance;

Denmark sends a mini-sub to a war in the desert;
Landlocked Switzerland wins the America's Cup...

The world is changing, never mind the prospects for stem-cell research, the spread of broadband Internet, over one billion Chinese in the market economy, and space travel. And it goes without saying that companies find themselves forced to change – a lot. In recent decades companies have started to pamper their customers and employees (some, at least), to appreciate the charms of technology and to love the Internet. And change is coming faster than ever. A couple of facts: The number of international phone calls a day in 2001 was equal to the total for the entire year of 1981;[25] in 2002 ABB, the Swedish-Swiss engineering giant, lost 68 percent of its market capitalization – a whopping five billion euros – in one week.[26]

Change, change, and more change. Change is necessary. It is a means of growing, of not getting bogged down and of staying on the crest of the wave. In organizations, however, the need for change crashes head on into a classic form of resistance: the fear of change. We are all its victims, in one way or another. And the reason is simple: our capacity to assimilate change is limited. If we could hop into a time machine and travel into the sort of science fiction future seen in *Blade Runner* or *Minority Report*, we would most likely be rather frightened, no matter how taken we might be with the cool gadgets (or with Tom Cruise himself). Change knocks us off stride: it deprives us of the control we need, and our insecurities can put us in checkmate.

> It is better to fail in originality than to succeed in imitation.
>
> Herman Melville, writer and
> author of *Moby Dick* (1819–1891)

I'll Take Habit

Monday morning football talk, the way to present reports, how we get more resources out of the budget manager – these are just a few of the endless habits or behavioral patterns we cultivate on the job and which change may jeopardize. And, what's worse, it is precisely on these habits that our feelings of security depend. If they are broken, we feel like Robinson Crusoe lost in a sea of doubts. Obviously, not everyone shares the same degree of reticence, nor are all changes of equal importance. Changing boss is not the same as changing stationery, despite all the grumbling about having to use recycled paper.

> They say that man is an animal of habit, but rather than of habit man is an animal.
>
> Mafalda, comic strip character
> created by Quino

They say that *man is an animal of habit* (although Mafalda has another view). And it's true. Habits free our brains from mechanical tasks and let us focus on more creative things at work, with friends or when making love, even if some have to reach for the *Kamasutra* to get beyond the missionary position.

Einstein always wore the same-style shirts and trousers to save time in choosing what to wear. An eminently practical idea, although it's not likely that Valentino, Jennifer López, and David Beckham would choose him for a role model. If we spent as much time thinking about what to have for breakfast as we do in designing a project, we would always be late for work. And if we took as long to decide the best way to get to the office as we do in picking a restaurant for dinner, we'd arrive even later. According to the psychologist

John McWhirter,[27] an expert on the subject, habits act upon the unconscious and we are more prone to be *hypnotized* than we think. If you are not convinced, how often do you actually think about shifting gears in the car? Of course, we are not talking about when you first sat behind the wheel and every move seemed like a do-or-die situation.

> Habits enable us to make room for doing other things.
> John McWhirter,
> psychologist specialized in habits

The Mafalda Philosophy

> People do not dislike change, but being changed.
> Paul Evans, Insead professor

The new boss is has arrived. He sums up the first meeting with a cryptic: "There are going to be changes around here." People are nervous. They hardly know what to expect from him. *Someone* knows *someone* that worked with him at another company. "He's tough," they say. "I heard that at the last company he sacked 20% of the staff. We haven't met our objectives in the last two years, maybe that's why he's here... ." Rumors start flying around the office. Nobody knows what to believe or how to deal with the new boss in person. Fear starts to take hold of the company, which, of course, no one acknowledges openly.

Fear of change is "like a box of chocolates; you never know what you're going to get," to paraphrase Forrest Gump. Within this fear we find the other fears we have identified: the fear for survival, the fear of rejection, the fear of failure, and the fear of loss of power. The arrival of a new boss with the smell of dismissal about him sets off the alarm of the first fear: not making it through the month. If there is to be reorganization in the division, some people will be changing departments; which activates the fear of rejection among new colleagues who neither know nor have developed trust in each other. If he is going to set new, tougher objectives, the fear of failure (a real drama for some) will rear its head. And if he is going to relieve someone of certain responsibilities, the fear of loss of power may strike.

So the fear of change may be as multifaced as it is disturbing and no wonder some feel like shouting: *Stop the world, I want to get off!*

Tips for Heightening the Fear of Change

If you want to utterly hamstring productivity in your company, here are some tips on how to create an acute fear of change:

1. *Uncertainty.* The less they know, the better. People need information like they need air. According to psychologists, we are *informavores*[28] (information-eaters). If we do not get it from the right source (or if it is partial, slanted, or manipulating), we look for it from the best alternative source: rumors. Rumors occur in direct proportion to the opacity of the organization. Another good way to create uncertainty is to leak out news of some alarming event – a possible merger, for example – without letting people know when it will happen.
2. *Change that goes against my own interests.* If you are going to outsource a department, don't expect the good will of the people involved, notwithstanding your assurances that they will be relocated. A well-known American consumer products multinational had the "brilliant idea" of

concentrating their management development in Boston, so that managers from Chile, Turkey, and Sweden would all be trained with the same methods and cultural sensitivities. In preparing this new team, the company sought ideas from the department head from each country, who knew that their position would probably be terminated (a nice way to say they would be sacked). It goes without saying what sort of brainstorming they got – more storm than brains.

3. *Unaccustomed to change.* If this is September, it must be time for change. That could be the maxim at many companies that have the compulsive need to make structural changes at the start of the fiscal year. And this is healthy, no argument there: it is a way of regenerating oneself. Workers at such companies are used to returning from the summer holidays to receive news of relocation. These changes explain why starting in June many sit on their hands waiting for their new assignment. Nontraumatic experiences diminish fear. But, if you want to compound fear, take your employees by surprise with your changes, and see what the consequences are. Moreover, next time, when they remember those changes, you will have achieved an even higher level of fear. People learn by association. If in the past something bad happened around this time of year, we can expect the same now.

4. *Belief that a change is not good for the company.* Finally, when a change is perceived as being bad for the company and, ultimately, for the person concerned, noticeable resistance will emerge. Perhaps we all like to play at being boss, imagining how we would run the company. So it is easy to understand how, for a responsible employee, a change that is bound to have a negative

impact on, say, customer services or product quality will be a motive for resistance.

> The greatest difficulty in the world is not for people to accept new ideas, but to make them forget their old ideas.
>
> John Maynard Keynes,
> economist (1883–1946)

KEYS TO FEARS À LA CARTE

- **Two sides of the same coin:** *Fear* mobilizes us when we face danger; *motivation* moves us to attain an objective. To know the motivation is to know the fear.

- **Five groups of fears:** Of not surviving (not making it through the month), of rejection, of failure, of the loss of power, and of change. Each group encompasses another set of fears.

- **Fear of not making it through the month:** Its impact on our lives depends on how vulnerable one is to losing one's job, how difficult it is to find another, financial needs, and training.

- **Fear of rejection:** Rooted in the need to belong to group. It is more acute in the Latin cultures and in young people. Sufferers seek the approval of peers, and standing out or being different is frowned upon.

- **Fear of failure:** Rooted in achievement motivation. It is particularly strong in companies and in Protestant cultures. Manifests itself in the drive to overachieve and to meet objectives set by others.

- **The fear of loss of power**: Rooted in the need to influence others. Although not acknowledged openly, perhaps the most important fear at the management level.

- **Fear of change**: The "mother" of all fears. Rooted in uncertainty, the fear of loss of control, and the inertia of habit.

3

THE PRICE OF FEAR

Welcome to the real world.

The Matrix, 1999

ALLIED, ALIENATED, OR ALIEN?

Cartier with Soy Sauce

For Cartier the battlefield is not only in the jewelers' showcases uptown, but overseas in hundreds of Chinese homes, too. Piracy is now a hot item in the land that gave us pasta, paper, and gunpowder. Churning out imitation watches at the startling rate of 100 to 150 a day, a family can eke out a living of 100 dollars a week. In the shop the copies go for $135, and are now available over the Internet, when the real thing might go as high as 3,000 euros. In a global world, competition (legal or otherwise) is global, too.[1]

We are riding the rollercoaster of uncertainty. Competitors from all over the globe saturate the markets. The average American supermarket stocks 40,000 different products. To satisfy 80 percent of its basic needs the average family needs just 150 different products.[2] In such circumstances, pressure is standard fare in companies: pressure to meet targets, pressure not to fail, pressure to hang on to your job. This pressure is inevitable, but we have tools with which to control it. Basically, we have two choices: management based on fear or management based on talent, change, and innovation.

Fifty percent of executives admit that their company promotes fear as a means of obtaining objectives (Figure 3.1). That is the finding of a survey of 185 middle managers and executives.[3] How many of them would have admitted that openly? The same study shows "casually" that organizations which focus on the potential of their employees keep fear in check. And, more interestingly, talent-based companies get the results they expect from their employees. No wonder. The part of the brain that activates when we are creative or enjoy our job is not the same one that lights up when fear strikes.[4] Like person, like company: in either case, we can either opt for the dark shadows of fear or fight to develop our potential and defy our own limits (see Table 3.1).

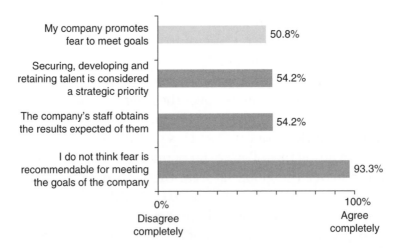

Figure 3.1 Love impossible: Fear and talent

Table 3.1   Fear versus talent, change, and innovation

Fear-based management is effective when:	Management based on Talent, Change, and Innovation is effective when:
Competition is predictable	Competition is unpredictable
Markets are stable	Markets are unstable
Customers have no choice	Customers have free choice
All work in the company is routine	Innovation and creativity are needed
Employees need only obey	All employees' potential is needed
Employees are robots	Employees are creative

Source: The author.

Tony Manero or the Duracell Bunny?

Fear is the classic management tool in companies. And let's give credit where credit is due: it has worked. When the market is stable and customers obedient, employees can act like robots, working mindlessly (or becoming alienated, in Marxist terminology) on production lines and behind desks. And they can save their creativity for their hobbies and friends. This is the *Saturday Night Fever* syndrome: life begins and ends at the weekend. The rest of the week is just to be got through.

However, competition changes the tune in the market. The company has to step to a new beat. Time to look for hidden talent and to ask your employees to act like John Travolta in the movie, not like the Duracell bunny. There's no room for fear on this dance floor. Do you want employees working toward a common goal? Ban fear. Want employees with the capacity to make decisions and committed to your customers? Ban fear. Want a business able to reinvent itself with each new change? Stamp fear's passport *"BANNED."*

> Business organizations can be the road to happiness for their people, but they can also be torture racks.
> Javier Fernández Aguado,
> professor and writer

You have got two choices: allied or alienated employees? (Because aliens don't seem to have much of a place in the company.) It is a question of returns. Depending on your market and your vision of the future (and personal principles, in some cases), you can either use fear as a management tool or give it the boot. If you want help, you might like to know about a study of management style and financial performance at sixty leading American companies. The authors, Raj Sisodia, Jag Sheth, and David Wolfe, found that those organizations led by "CEOs that inspire respect, loyalty and even affection, rather than fear," had returned 758 percent over 10 years, compared with 128 percent for the Standard & Poor's 500.[5] And another fact: only 36 percent of employees state that they put their full potential into their work.[6] Can you imagine the returns if the figure was up near 100 percent?

> People are ready for a workplace without fear.
> Kathleen Ryan and Daniel Oestreich,
> authors of *Driving Fear Out of the Workplace*

CUSTOMERS WITH BRAND TATTOOS

Motorized Muscles

If you tattooed the Harley Davidson logo on your arm, you would enter the select group of the company's truest customers.[7] And that would be no mean commitment. A tattoo is for life, maybe not for as long as a diamond, but much longer than a marriage, of course.[8] We are living in an era of brand veneration. Some lucky names have reached near-religious status among their most ardent fans, as in the cases of Harley Davidson and Nike (whose followers have also been known to sport a tattoo of the famous swoosh).[9] And the brand, like all the illusions that surround it, is intangible.

> In the factory we make cosmetics; in the drugstore we sell hope.
>
> Charles Revson, founder of Revlon

Hope it is, of course. Revson was quite aware that good marketing and eye-catching photos produced miracles. That is the magic of advertising – and of intangibles, which are not an issue just in marketing. Ninety-five percent of the universe is made up of invisible matter. We fall in love due to pheromones we cannot see (Oh, if the Bard were to hear that!). A third of the cost of a Boeing 777 is software.[10] For the average product, R+D, logistics, and employee training eat up a much fatter slice of investment than manufacturing. In cars, materials account for just 16 percent of the total price.[11] The competition is so fierce and products are so easy to copy that the only way to differentiate yourself is with intangibles. In the United States alone companies invest 233 billion dollars a year in advertising, six times what the country spends on education.[12] And each company is trying to find its mystique in the invisible.

BMW tempts us with the pleasure of driving on smooth roads free of traffic (does such a thing actually exist?). Nike instills in us the idea that there are no limits: *Just do it*, though we only wear their clothes to watch TV slumped on the sofa. L'Oreal offers us a free blast of self-esteem with no need to see a psychologist: *Because I'm worth it*. Intangibles fill the voids in our lives; they are the stuff of dreams. And dreams are the bait companies use to hook customers. In a world without competition, companies would not "waste" money on marketing strategies or product personalization. Nor would they bother with the intangibles that are meant to act as aphrodisiacs on customers. Nor would they care about the potential of their employees, who in the end are ones who turn eyeliner into hopes, as our friend Mr. Revson would say.

Winning Matches (Customers) to Win the League (Market Share)

> No longer can the critical resources of a firm be touched (at least not without risking a lawsuit for sexual harassment).
>
> Jonas Ridderstråle and Kjell Nordström,
> authors of *Karaoke Capitalism*

The competition has thrown down the gauntlet and it is with our brains that we must do battle. Brute force, once so sought after, is now relegated to the humble rank of squire. The premium is now on gray matter. And that is what organizations want from the ground up (Figure 3.2). The aim is clear: to succeed in the *moments of truth*, as Jan Carlzon would say.[13]

Personalized attention: a flight attendant with a Colgate smile kindly helping a passenger to store her bag. In the advert that is the way it goes, but the *moment of truth* comes when we press the call button on the armrest and the flight attendant appears with a haughty look on his face, if he bothers to glance in our direction at all. When Carlzon was

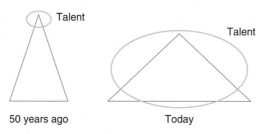

Figure 3.2 Talent: Something new?
Source: The author.

named president of SAS (Scandinavian Airline Systems) in 1981, the company was a minor player among the European carriers. In less than ten years he turned it into one of the top airlines on the continent. He achieved that feat by managing properly the moments of truth: in other words, those instances when a customer comes into contact with a person who represents the firm. "Last year," he says, "each of our 10 million customers came in contact with approximately five SAS employees, and this contact lasted an average of 15 seconds each time, and each of those moments determined whether the company would succeed or fail."

> Everything has been done a thousand times, but everything must be invented in each battle, because the possibilities for individual expression are unlimited.
>
> Sun Tzu, general and author
> of *The Art of War* (500 AD)

Military strategists hold that wars are won in each battle. In sport, coaches follow the same creed: to be the champion you have to take each match as if it were your last. The same goes for companies. While the ultimate goal is market share, you achieve that customer by customer – in each moment of truth. And in order to deal successfully with those moments, you need customer-oriented employees with initiative and the capacity to make decisions.

The Price We Pay

But everything has its price. Our competitors have done us a favor. Thanks to competitive pressure, companies started to concern themselves with the talent of their employees – no mean feat for organizations hooked on fear-based management. However, also thanks to competition we now suffer other more subtle fears. It seems ironic: what saved us from mind-numbing routine drives us back into the tunnel of fear. And we have only just begun.

Just 20 percent of world production is open to global competition, according to the consultants McKinsey & Company. In thirty years that figure will reach 80 percent.[14] One day of foreign currency exchange in 2000 equaled the entire year's total for 1979.[15] The competitive pressure is greater than ever. Once, you knew who your competitors were; now, under the new rules, they may come from next door or the other side of the globe. In a world without borders and with the aid of technology, the big players can make a killing in markets in many countries; and, when a multinational moves in, it can knock the locals for a loop. And the duel may be between titans (as when Canon took on Xerox), a giant against an army of mortals (Arla Foods, the European powdered-milk multinational, against local dairymen in the Dominican Republic) or between David and Goliath (the upstart Dell versus IBM). Whatever the case, market instability aggravates the fear of losing competitiveness, power, and of course, jobs.

However, there is another giant, a sleeping giant which is just only beginning to stir. One of every five inhabitants of our planet is Chinese. Labor costs in China are highly competitive and the people's capacity for work is not just a cliché. Very soon, China will be rewriting the global rules. It has already started. In late 2004, Lenovo bought IBM's personal computers division for 1.3 billion euros, the biggest ever overseas takeover by a Chinese firm. The new company became the third largest in the world, after Dell and Hewlett Packard.[16] In Colombia the Chinese were the first to sell low-price domestic appliances.[17] They are now breaking into the European car market with a line starting below 5,000 euros. In Spain they have snatched a huge market share away from the textile and shoe industries. And this is only the beginning. In a few years we will be witnessing a fascinating battle with a "sweet and sour" flavour. With this outlook, uncertainty, with its attendant fears, lies just below the surface. Let's talk about other consequences of competition: sackings and the pressure to work longer hours.

FOLLOWING THE FADS OF THE ORACLES

To Be There or Not to Be There. That Is the Question

> History repeats itself; that's one of the things that's wrong with history.
>
> Charles Darwin (1809–1882)

Downsizing causes heart attacks, even among those who keep their jobs. That is the chilling conclusion of a study done in Finland over seven and a half years with a sample of 22,000 nonmanual workers.[18] According to the study, the "lucky ones" left over after a major downsizing (a greater than 18 percent cut in the workforce) suffer higher rates of sickness absence and, what's worse, their probabilities of dying from cardiac arrest multiply fivefold over the next four years. Why? The authors of the study point out two: on the one hand, the severe stress and uncertainty about being the next in line to lose one's job; on the other hand, the fact that fewer people had to do the same amount of work.

The study examined municipal workers in four Finnish towns in a period of economic recession. Employing the classic cost-cutting recipe, the towns downsized their work-forces, despite the fact that there had been no drop either in population or in the demand for municipal services. Obviously, one needn't travel to Finland to see that these sorts of measures are no exception to the rule. Sometimes major downsizing may be necessary, but the "collateral damage" often exceeds anticipations (when there are any anticipations), and the results often fall short. At least that is what was found in the study by consultants Watson Wyatt. Of 1,005 companies that had downsized between 1986 and 1991, they found that only 46 percent said the measure was justified in terms of cost-savings; 36 percent were happy with the rise in profits, and just 14 percent could cite an improvement in customer satisfaction.[19]

The reasons for downsizing are manifold, as Jaime Bonache[20] points out: cost-cutting, mergers, technological advances – even the unfortunate "follow-the-leader" effect. In the latter case, it is the *great oracles*, the strategic consultants and their clients, who are the guest starts in our next horror film.

The Fads of the Oracles

> My Interest is in the future because I am going to spend the rest of my life there.
>
> Charles Kettering, American engineer, inventor of the electric starter

The lost city of Delphi, with its Oracle, located in the shadow of Mount Parnassus and surrounded by sacred springs, was the main religious center of the Hellenic world. To the temple of Delphi leaders made pilgrimages to receive the wise counsel of the priestess of Apollo, whose power derived from divine vapors emanating from a crack in the floor in the inner sanctum. The priestess sat on a three-legged stool over the crack and answered the governors' questions with cryptic messages, which would then have to be deciphered. A lovely story, but one which has recently lost much of its mystery. Jelle Zeilinga de Boer, a geology professor at Wesleyan University in Connecticut, found that the area where the temple once stood lies over a geological fault. And it appears that the inspirational "divine vapors" were, in fact, methane and ethane gases which simply put the priestess into a delirious state.[21] So much for the myth.

The term oracle remains part of our language today, and in the business world it is used to refer to the top strategic consultants and their main clients. Their recommendations, without doubt founded on in-depth research and methods quite different from those of the priestesses of Delphi, set the trends for their clients and, due to the knock-on effect, those of other companies.

Back in the 1980s size was the way to go. IBM was the prime example of the management model to imitate. "Its size is its key to success," exclaimed the *Financial Times* in 1992.[22] Several years later, it seemed that the company's bulk was making it as competitive as the woolly mammoth in the late Pleistocene era. The oracles then preached re-engineering and companies began to sharpen the knives of downsizing. Next the world fell in love with the Internet and the oracles warned that it was crucial to be on the web of webs. In one case, a hotel chain was informed that its true mission was online bed sales, and that only for purposes of appearance did it need to maintain its hotel business.

Of course, for years now the oracles have been touting globalization as a basic strategy for achieving cost efficiency. This means moving not only manufacturing to countries with cheaper labor, but services too. If you have a question about a bill, you pick up the phone and someone thousands of miles away fields your call. Meanwhile, power is being centralized, a trend (or fad, only time will tell) that is tying the hands of managers out in the field, who now see the word "dispensable" each time they look in the mirror. We will have to be on the lookout for the oracles' next great revelation. Until then, fear is the order of the day, and happiness will just have to take a back seat.

Time, the Scarce Resource

> The difference between Zeltia and its competitors is that we could afford to wait. Being the majority shareholder and company chairman, I don't have the pressure for immediate returns that other CEOs live with. That's why we could invest in the long term.
>
> José Fernández Sousa Faro, President of Zeltia

Today, how long does the average company president or managing director last in their job (not counting family businesses, of course)? The answer is quite revealing in terms of time pressure. The West is leading the world away from the Japanese model of high job security in an alarming trend toward the revolving door policy. Thirty-five of the Fortune 100 companies replaced their CEOs between 1995 and 2000.[23] It is not surprising then how some multinationals boast of how long their top executives have been on board, as in the case of General Electric, the world's largest corporation in terms of market capitalization. In its nearly 100 years of history, GE has had just twelve presidents. Its last CEO, Jack Welch, held the post for a record-breaking twenty years.

Time pressure it is not without costs. It is one of the prices of the growing competition. In a world driven by consumption, consumers demand new products faster (or, rather, they are sucked in by ever more newfangled goods). Zara, the chain of clothing shops owned by the Spanish multinational Inditex, is a prime example. From the design of a new garment to placing it on the rack – indeed, to renew its entire collection – it takes Zara all of ten to fifteen days.[24]

> Twenty percent of our company's technical knowledge becomes obsolete each year.
> Bill Joy, chief scientist at Sun Microsystems

The byword in marketing is change. Customers want it. We need it! Sometimes compulsively. A credit card, a shopping center and a bruised self-esteem make the perfect combination for running your bank account into the red. But perhaps the most interesting thing about time pressure is its role in generating fears and personal dissatisfaction. We are constantly pressed to meet tighter and tighter deadlines. Sun Microsystems does sales forecasts and revises management objectives on a weekly basis. Cisco Systems closes its books every day. Not so long ago strategic plans were for five years. Today it is hard, if not impossible, to define strategies for more than a year. And it looks like time is going to become only scarcer. While in the past decade the auto industry cut the time it takes from the design of a new car to its release by 30 percent[25] (from three years to two, roughly) and the goal in the Japanese industry is to reduce that period to less than a year. In short, everything must be done by yesterday. And this pressure spawns fears which, in the end, lead only to frustration.

> We live increasingly in a nanosecond culture.
> Jeremy Rifkin, president of the Foundation
> on Economic Trends in Washington

As an anecdote, this nanosecond culture has engendered its own resistance movement in the form of the *slow life* creed. This movement first appeared in Rome in the mid-1980s, sparked by a protest against the opening of a fast food restaurant on the famed stairs of the Piazza di Spagna. The original aim to promote a more relaxed style of eating – *slow food* – subsequently ballooned into an organization that claims over seventy-five thousand members today.[26] Slow cities and schools without bells are two of its projects. The Italian town of Bra, with fifteen thousand inhabitants, has imposed a maximum speed limit of 20kph on its streets; the Martin Luther King School in Berkeley, California, has an "edible schoolyard" where the students grow, and watch grow, much of their own food. Still, although such alternative ideas for escaping the tyranny of the clock have their merits, they remain far from offering a valid solution in the business world – unless, of course, you want to be steamrolled by the competition.

BULLETS OF FEAR

Our environment, as we know, generates more subtle fears. But companies have the challenge of dealing with them, rather than using them as a weapon. Fear-based management is like a sniper: it puts a bullet through the heart of change, innovation, and employee potential. If you are determined to go this way, you should know the casualties (Figure 3.3)

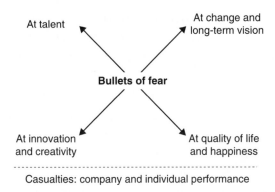

Figure 3.3 Bullets of fear
Source: The author.

Requiem for Talent

> Fear invites wrong figures.
> Edward Deming, quality guru (1900–1993)

Which car would you buy: one that needs three or four repairs in the first year or one that needs just one repair or even zero? Naturally, there is no question there, as the U.S. auto industry discovered in the 1970s, when Americans swallowed their patriotic pride and started buying Japanese cars by the millions. We have already hinted at the reason. In 1977, Hertz Rent-A-Car did a study of the number of trips to the garage for each hundred cars in its fleet. Ford and Chevrolet scored 326 and 425, respectively, while for Toyota the rate was just 55. That difference had its origin in a process that had begun in Japanese industry in the fifties, and, irony of ironies, thanks to an American, Edwards Deming.[27]

Deming is the father of quality, and he received from Emperor Hirohito the Sacred Treasure Medal in 1960 in recognition of the good he had done for the country. Deming's formula for quality, which proved so successful in Japan, contains fourteen points – nine of which relate to fear.[28] According to Deming, fear neutralizes motivation and the ability to reflect. Research on the human brain supports his theory, as we have seen. When we use our potential, our neuronal connections interact happily. When fear invades our inner being, it sequesters those connections, along with our talent – and saps our ability to lead and to take the initiative. Under such circumstances we are hardly likely to deal successfully with those moments of truth. An employee who is afraid only looks to please the boss.

When fear walks in the door, talent flies out the window.

In addition, remember another thing: innovation occurs where people breathe freely, where mistakes are not met with punishment and suggestions for improvement are welcome. People are creative by nature. We just need the right environment and objectives to shoot for. When people believe in us (and we believe in ourselves) we exceed our own limits. If the organization creates the right atmosphere, the rest will follow, even if you are a dark horse in the land of Henry Ford. The first casualty of fear: your employees' talent.

> People will be more creative when they feel motivated primarily by the interest, enjoyment, satisfaction and challenge of the work itself rather than external pressure.
> Edward Deming, quality guru (1900–1993)

By the way, in 1980 the U.S. network NBC TV broadcast a report called If Japan Can, Why Can't We. It was then that Deming first became a household name in his own country, and thanks to television, because Deming had been writing articles and giving talks for nearly thirty years.[29] Perhaps the old saying really is true: no one is a prophet in their own land.

Fear = Short-Sightedness

> One cannot manage change. One can only be ahead of it.
> Peter Drucker, writer and
> corporate management guru

In 1865 Fredrik Idestam, a Finnish mining engineer, opened a paper mill, later expanding into rubber tyres, footwear, and rainwear. One hundred and thirty-three years later, in 1998, the company became the world leader in its sector – which was no longer paper or rubber, but mobile phones (or cell phones, as our friends across the pond call them). Of course we are talking about Nokia. At the dawn of the twenty-first century the company controlled 27 percent of the world market, employed over 55,000 people in forty-five countries, and was admired as one of the most innovative companies on the planet. Not bad for a centenarian company from a small town in a country of five million inhabitants.[30]

Nokia is a prime example of an organization that since its founding has known how to move with the times. How many companies as old as Nokia have managed to reinvent themselves and re-emerge to be world leaders? What's Nokia's secret? Adapt to change and reinvent oneself. Fear, however, blinds us to the future. We cling to the past, for the future could only be worse, and thus we cannot possibly reinvent anything.

> One of my personality traits is that when I analyze a change I focus more on the advantages for the future than on what I may lose.
> José Cabrera, former president of
> Sun Microsystems Iberia

Fear = Short-sightedness. That might be a good way to summarize the impact. An employee who is afraid is incapable of seeing beyond the threat. And perhaps one of the key traits of successful entrepreneurs or innovators is that they focus on what they stand to gain rather than what they stand to lose. As the joke goes: Optimist or misinformed pessimist? But Dr. Martin Seligman has studied this dichotomy and found that optimists process more information from their surroundings than do pessimists, who see only the dark side.[31] And it goes without saying that backward-looking organizations are easy prey for their competitors. Fear's second casualty: change and long-term vision.

Our Reserved Creativity

> We usually find oil in a new place with old ideas. Sometimes, we find oil in an old place with a new idea, but we seldom find much oil in an old place with an old idea. Several times in the past we have thought that we were running out of oil, when actually we were running out of ideas.
>
> Parke Atherton Dickey, professor,
> University of Tulsa, Oklahoma

The Nokia story may sound like a fairy tale; and indeed it does, desperate moments of truth and all. Not so long ago, the company was on the verge of going under. After a string of bad years, in 1991 Nokia's major shareholder, a bank, offered to sells its shares to the Swedish competitor Ericsson, who turned them down.[32] Later, when Nokia began to gobble up the Swedes' market share, Ericsson's board of directors must have wondered how they could have missed such a golden opportunity. From that moment, the Nokia story took a new turn. The company managed to overtake the giant Motorola on its own ground, the United States. And the roots of such success lie in a capacity for innovation.

In the early nineties, the Nokia mobile phones were hardly the hot item. The technology was good, but they weighed twice as much as the new Japanese models. Then Jorma Ollila, company president and managing director, decided to go back to the drawing table (signing research agreements with universities all over the world) and turn the mobile phone into an "object of desire." With that idea in mind, they came out with a new phone loaded with extras: display with options menu, interchangeable bodies, personalized tones, and sundry other bells and whistles. They offered each customer the possibility of making their phone their own. And it was a whopping success. Nokia took the lead, and dictated the trends, in the market. In 2001, the normally staid Financial Times wrote: "Ericsson last year lost 2.3 million dollars on mobile phone devices because their products are ugly."[33] Today in the mobile phone industry everybody loves design.

> Fifteen years agocompanies competed on price, now it's quality, tomorrow it's design.
> Robert Hayes, Harvard Business School professor

In 2001 Nokia was the fifth most admired company in the world, surpassed only by Coca-Cola, Microsoft, IBM, and GE, and the only European firm in the top 10, according to an annual Business Week study.[34] In 2005 it was still a well-deserved sixth. Nokia saw the way to make mobile phones sexy, though the company later lost market share. The competition is fierce in such an appetizing market. Its rivals are following its lead in the drive to innovate and it is not easy to identify the trends and technologies that are going to triumph in the future. But, nonetheless, we can extract a lesson from the Nokia story: innovation paves the way to the top, and fear is the nemesis of innovation.

> Creativity is the destination, but courage is the journey.
> Joey Reiman, creativity expert and author
> of *Thinking for a Living*

We create through interaction. Bacteria grow by exchanging information in the form of DNA. As the Nokia story shows, innovation is the product of the joint efforts of various teams. Even the Renaissance was the product of different schools of the arts rather than isolated geniuses. But in order to set this process in motion, first you need the right physical and emotional environment.

> We shape our buildings, and afterwards our buildings shape us.
> Winston Churchill,
> British prime minister (1874–1965)

Steelcase, an office furnishings maker, has come up with what it calls the "flexible office": designs that adapt to the needs of the team. The flexible office serves as an individual workspace as well as for meetings, so employees needn't gather around the coffeemaker to have a chat with their colleagues. But the system requires an open floor plan: no stranded islets, no static cubicles, which create claustrophobia rather than creativity. Nor can this be done with robotic employees who need the boss's approval, nor with a management style fraught with threats. Let's be clear about it. Creativity is too "demure" to prosper under such conditions, and fear is not exactly its best suitor. Now we come to the third casualty of fear: innovation and creativity.

Tomorrow I'll Be Happy

> While we have created every kind of labor- and time-saving device and activity [...] we are beginning to feel like we have less time available to us than any other humans in history.
>
> Jeremy Rifkin, president of the Foundation
> on Economic Trends in Washington

Do you put off leisure for work? Do you sacrifice your sleep? These are some of the symptoms of the fear of not achieving objectives – a condition that has now become a widespread illness. It is known as the deferred happiness syndrome (DHS), and it affects 40 percent of full-time workers in developed countries, according to an Australian study.[35] Let's have a look at the symptoms:

1. Do you work harder and longer hours in order to support a comfortable lifestyle (home, car, schools, holidays)?
2. Do you feel the need to save all you can for a possibly idealized retirement?
3. Are you afraid of changing jobs, preferring to endure the stress you live with?

DHS has a number of consequences. On the one hand, happiness in the present is sacrificed to long hours of hard work in the belief that everything will change for the better in the future. On the other hand, the fear of losing one's security means one is unable to take risks. If I allow myself certain luxuries now, I may endanger my quality of life in the future. Then only health problems or professional or personal crisis can force the person to seek alternatives. This is also true at the company level. I cannot invest in the future if that means diverting resources from my present endeavors! I have to remain focused on the present objectives and keep my nose to the grindstone every day! Meanwhile, I'm sacrificing my quality of life and, if I am a business, my competitiveness, too.

However, there is another casualty of the deferred happiness syndrome: the kids who during the week barely see their parents other than in family photos. Of course their parents work hard to provide them with the quality of life they consider appropriate. As one executive said: "I work and travel a lot, but l do it for my son. That way my wife doesn't have to work and my son can spend more time with his mother." But children prefer more time with *both* parents over other sorts of favors, according to a study by B. Pocock and J. Clark.[36] The children they interviewed were aware of their parents' sacrifices, but at the same time they said that when they became parents they would devote more time to their children rather than to the pursuit of a successful career. We'll just have to wait and see.

> While it takes weeks to chemically treat cancer, burn-out takes much longer to treat.
>
> Leif Edvinsson, professor
> from the University of Lun, Sweden

You needn't suffer from DHS to know that fear is a deadly foe of your happiness and quality of life. Over the last fifty years in the developed countries purchasing power has multiplied several times, but rates of happiness remain the same and, what's worse, the incidence of depression has shot up tenfold.37 Our happiness is lying in the intensive care unit: antiulcerants and antidepressants are two of the hottest-selling drugs in the world.[38] Stress and sadness, in other words. The top-selling drugs reduce the cholesterol caused by eating too much of the wrong foods. In a world where half the population suffers from hunger, the other half has to take drugs because they eat too much fat. And fears make us more prone to illness and to "let life pass by", instead of seizing it by the horns.

Dr. Elisabeth Kubler-Ross,[39] who worked with terminally ill patients for nearly forty years, wrote that we regret two things before dying: not having made amends with someone, usually a family member, and not having dared to do more things. If it were not for our fears, how much more would we achieve? Fourth casualty of fear: our quality of life and our happiness.

> To be happy is to be able to become aware of oneself without fright.
>
> Walter Benjamin, philosopher (1892–1940)

KEYS TO THE PRICE OF FEAR:

- **Two choices**: Employees can be managed on the basis of fear or on the basis of talent, change, and innovation. Which is better? It depends on the market and what the sort of future the company wants.

- **Thank you, competition**: Competitive pressure has shifted more importance to the intangibles and to the talents of the workers – who are the ones who attract customers and make the company stand out among the competition.

- **But**: Competitive pressure also generates more subtle fears, related to sackings, uncertainty, and tight deadlines.

- **Casualties of fear-based management**: The use of fear in companies kills off:
  - Employees' talent
  - Change and long-term vision
  - Innovation and creativity
  - Quality of life and happiness

4

THE CHALLENGE FOR *NOFEAR* ORGANIZATIONS

> The battlefield is also accordingly here – within ourselves and our institutions.
>
> John Dewey,
> philosopher (1859–1952)

A FRAMEWORK FOR THE CHALLENGE

How Fear Is Transmitted in the Company

A group of scientists put five monkeys in a cage, at the center of which they placed a ladder with a bunch of bananas hanging above. When one of the monkeys climbed the ladder to get at the bananas, the scientists sprayed the others with cold water. After a while, whenever a monkey tried to climb the ladder, the others would drag it back down and beat it. In the end, none of them would dare climb the ladder, despite the temptation of the bananas. Then, the scientists replaced one of the monkeys.

The first thing the newcomer did was to try to climb the ladder; the others reacted as they had before. After a few beatings, the newcomer stopped trying to get at the bananas. Another monkey was replaced and the same thing happened. And the first substitute joined enthusiastically in the beating dished out to the new arrival. A third monkey was replaced and the story repeated itself, and so on until the last of the original members of the group was gone.

The scientists were now left with a group of five monkeys none of which had received the cold-water treatment. But they still beat up on any monkey that made an attempt to get the bananas. Were it possible to ask them why they would not let any of their number climb the ladder, the answer would most likely have been something like: "I don't know, that's the way it's always been around here."

> Culture transmits not only the fear but the form as well.
> Enrique Luque, professor,
> Universidad Autónoma de Madrid

So, here we have a group of sore, hungry monkeys and a bunch of bananas that none will eat. Can a company afford to have this sort of situation? We have been running on fear for a long time. And although there is only a 4-percent difference between the human and the chimpanzee genomes,[1] people – and companies – have the wherewithal for change, for shaping a different future. Companies can choose more sophisticated, more profitable methods – based on talent, change, and innovation. And they can break the *simian* inertia. Therein lies their great challenge.

> It is harder to crack a prejudice than an atom.
> Albert Einstein (1879–1955)

Table 4.1   Mechanisms for NoFear organizations

Mechanisms for action	Challenges for the NoFear organization
Company project	Balancing the efforts of the players
Power and authority	Serving the organization
Leadership	Developing leaders able to face up to their own fears
Management systems	Suitable for avoiding fear and promoting talent, innovation, and change
Communication	Communicate, communicate, and communicate some more

Sailors take warning: there is no perfect company, nor any magic formula. Many of our fears in the workplace we bring from home, others have their source in the organization (like when you were little, in your relationship with your siblings, friends, or fellow footballers). But companies can act. They have binary mechanisms: they can either promote or alleviate fear. One or the other. If a company opts for fear-based management, it is following the classic model. The company will not win any prizes for innovation (whether it can survive against the competition is another question). If the company settles for the second alternative, it must create a defensive wall (Figure 4.1) to fend off toxic fears and provide room for employees' potential. How? By using the appropriate mechanisms for building a **NoFear** organization (Table 4.1). And since there is no one recipe for success, the exact mechanisms and how they are applied will depend on each firm. Below we examine these mechanisms and the challenges they entail.

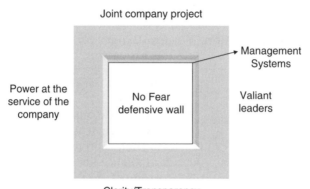

Figure 4.1 A defensive wall against fear

ESSENCE OR IMAGE?

Challenge: The company as a joint project

Managing Director by Election

> I understand the company as joint life project for the empowerment of all its participants.
>
> Pedro Luis Uriarte, president of Economía,
> Empresa, Estrategia

Can I choose my managing director? You can if you work for Mondragón Cooperative Corporation.[2] Mondragón was originally founded in the Spanish Basque Country in 1956, when five students decided to set up a stove factory, under the aegis of Padre José María Arizmendiarrieta, instigator of the project. Today Mondragón comprises 100 independent cooperatives and over 150 businesses (among them Fagor appliances, Irizar coachworks, and Eroski hypermarkets) and employs over 70,000 people in sixty-five countries.[3] Each worker-shareholder has a say in the running of the company, independently of his or her job and number of shares. The general shareholders' meeting elects a board which names the "managing directors" and division managers for a period of four years.

Mondragón's competitiveness is unquestionable. Among the kudos it has earned from the international business community, Fortune named it one of the ten best companies to work for in Europe,[4] along with companies like Ferrari, Bacardi, Martini, and Nestlé. The reason? Equality, individual capacity to make decisions, absence of a hierarchical atmosphere – all of which is set out in its mission:

> The Mondragón Cooperative Corporation (MCC) is a business-based socioeconomic initiative with deep roots in the Basque Country, created for and by people and inspired by the Basic Principles of our Cooperative Experience. It is firmly committed to the environment, competitive improvement and customer satisfaction in order to generate wealth in society through business development and the creation of, preferably cooperative, employment.

Mondragón is an exceptional case: it has been the object of study by the English-speaking press, and when Henry Mintzberg, one of the fathers of contemporary organizational theory, visited the company he suggested "mass producing Mondragóns all over the world."[5]

Balance of Forces ... the Most Difficult Part?

> Being an entrepreneur means sales figures, profitability. Being an entrepreneur means having a global vision of the business, spotting opportunities and risks. Being an entrepreneur is synonymous with returns.
>
> Magda Salarich, general director
of Citroen Spain

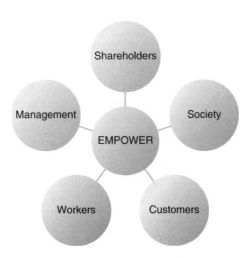

Figure 4.2 Balanced forces?
Source: The author.

The primary objective of any company: make money. How that is achieved depends on the company project. It matters not whether it sells clothing or condoms, or what the pretty mission statement on the website says. It is a question of the very essence of the company, the air breathed within it, something that only those on the inside know. We are talking about how the company conceives of the sharing of weight among its "stakeholders": shareholders, executives, employees, customers, and society. These five act like particles around an atom, applying different forces (Figure 4.2): sometimes seemingly contradictory (the shareholders earn more money if jobs are cut); other times complementary (the more motivated the workers, the better the service they give to customers and the higher the dividends for the shareholders).

The company project and the balance between the five stakeholders are decided by the owners or top executives. If you are not included among these chosen few, worry not.

You can promote **NoFear** from any position in the company. Depending on the project, powersharing will either be balanced, as in the case of Mondragón, where shareholder = executive = employee, or a few will benefit at the cost of the others – though powersharing is hardly an area that excels in originality.

Empowerment has the opposite effect of "enfearment." Empowerment is enriching; fear is debilitating. Could a toothpaste manufacturer take reprisals against consumers who switch brands? Could it do so against investors who disinvest? Hardly, although some may insist on trying. But what about your boss? He certainly can. When fear is used as a management tool it is usually applied to two of the stakeholders: workers and management (not top management, hopefully). It is rare that fear is wielded against shareholders, customers, or society. And the reasons for this lie in freedom of choice.

Employees are free in the sense that there is no law to prohibit them from looking for another job; but that is not as easy as switching brands of toothpaste. If it were that simple, as it was for some engineers during the Internet boom, fear as a management tool would be useless. Thus, when we talk about the company project we are talking about the concept of powersharing among the five stakeholders, especially employees and certain executives.

> We will have to redefine the purpose of the employing organization and of its management, to satisfy both the legal owners, such as shareholders, and the owners of the human capital that gives the organization its wealth-producing power, that is, the knowledge workers.
>
> Peter Drucker, writer and
> corporate management guru

Science Fiction in the Company

OUR VALUES[6]

- **Respect.** We treat others as we would like to be treated ourselves. We do not tolerate abusive or disrespectful treatment. Ruthlessness, callousness, and arrogance don't belong here.

- **Integrity.** We work with customers and prospects openly, honestly and sincerely. When we say we will do something, we will do it; when we say we cannot or will not do something, then we won't do it.

- **Communication.** We have an obligation to communicate. Here, we take the time to talk with one another ... and to listen. We believe that information is meant to move and that information moves people.

- **Excellence.** We are satisfied with nothing less than the very best in everything we do. We will continue to raise the bar for everyone. The great fun here will be for all of us to discover just how good we can really be.

Source: www.enron.com, October 1998.

Respect, integrity, communication, and excellence. Who wouldn't want to work for a company with these values? But the company that stated those values in its 1998 annual report was Enron. Enron was once a giant in the energy production and distribution sector. At its height it was the sixth biggest company in the United States in terms of turnover, an economic symbol in its home country and a favorite of the business press and researchers. But in late 2001 Enron filed for bankruptcy, brought on by the illicit practices of its top executives. It was one of the biggest scandals in business history. Nearly 22,000 people lost their jobs and shareholders lost 30 billion dollars, while twenty-nine executives had pocketed 1.1 billion in cash a few months before, when Enron was still a star on Wall Street.[7]

We won't get into all the details of the Enron story, which would make a fine thriller with a tragic ending, but one thing is clear: those executives acted in their own interests, not those of the company's shareholders, customers, or employees, nor of any other living being for that matter. Impeccable values, notwithstanding. By the way, after the company went under, some former employees began auctioning off on eBay all sorts of Enron paraphernalia (pins, employee-of-the-month awards, etc.) and one of the highest bids, $202.50, was for the *Ethics Code* booklet handed out to every worker.[8] Obviously some were quick to see that a disaster of that magnitude held at least some opportunity. What else could they do?

But Enron is just one, albeit stunning, example of how wide the chasm is between what a company says and what it does (although Enron might deserve an Oscar for its performance). Terms like "corporate social responsibility," "the environment," "business ethics," "customer" or "talent" fill the pages of company websites and the speeches given by their executives. Undoubtedly many companies and employees are indeed concerned with these issues, but many others are concerned only with their own image. In a world that places so much emphasis on prestige (of a company or whomever), it is hard not to follow the prevailing winds of fashion. But those on the inside know whether the pretty words are pure marketing or the expression of real concern.

The Million-Dollar Question

> All men are alikein their words; their actions only show them to be different.
>
> Molière, writer and playwright (1622–1673)

The million-dollar question: Is it possible to balance empowerment of your workers with that of the other stakeholders (shareholders, customers, top executives, and society)? Of course, it is. Admittedly, the task is not an easy one; nevertheless deeds, not talk, is the way to do it. At Mondragón job creation is part of the mission and the essence of the firm: *created for and by people.* In terms of pay scale, the highest paid person earns six times what the lowest paid person gets (performance bonuses apart). In the big American companies it was 40 times in 1980 and 400 in 1990 (the increase is due to the policy of lavishing stock options on top executives).[9] Interestingly, in *The Republic* Plato recommends that no man should earn over five times what the lowest worker receives. (Perhaps Mondragón found inspiration in Ancient Greece?) And Mondragón's egalitarian pay policy is not only internal; it is also on par with the rest of the labor market.

And how do you empower your employees? There are different ways to do so,[10] but perhaps the best place to start is with authority and power. Of course we are on slippery ground here, but this is where fear takes root. If you want a **NoFear** organization, you'll have to don the surgeon's mask and take the scalpel to your most delicate organ.

POWER: THE HEART OF FEAR

Challenge: Power at the service of the company

Fear the Stalker

> Punishment and fear are closely related and deeply rooted in the unconscious of the members of an organization.
>
> Steven Appelbaum, professor,
> Concordia University, Canada

The psychologist B. F. Skinner was the father of behaviorism. In broad terms, his theory is based on the supposition that our behavior is determined by reward and punishment;[11] the carrot and the stick, in other words. Everyone likes to receive a reward for the things they do well. The problem is in punishment (or penalty, to phrase it better). The function of punishment, according to Skinner, is to alter behavior. And someone who holds power can mete out punishment. If we want an IT technician to stop arriving late at the office, we can give him a ticking-off or threaten him with some sort of penalty. But this will work only if we outrank him in the company hierarchy. Logically, the threat would not be very effective if it came from the security guard at the gate:

Only a person with power can generate fear.

We needn't feel fear directly to know it is there. It must be one of the most contagious emotions there is! If we learn that a manager has lost his job because he did not get along well with the new president, even though we are not the one who has fallen out of favor, we suddenly become highly aware of the risk. Fear stalks us. The very hint of it and it invades our mind. Horror film directors are experts at exploiting fear, as are certain organizations and executives.

But at the same time we are free! Each of us deals with power according to our own circumstances. Evidently, someone who can easily find another job, or who naturally questions the rules will be less accommodating to authority. Some people who get traffic fines pay immediately in deference to authority (what some people call civil behavior) while others will forget them in a drawer somewhere until they turn brown with age (what we call uncivil behavior).

> Man is not fully conditioned and determined but rather determines himself.
>
> Viktor Frankl, psychiatrist and author
> of *Man's Search for Meaning* (1905–1997)

We Need Power...

One billion "customers," over one million "employees" and twenty centuries of history? The Catholic Church is undoubtedly one of the most successful organizations in history. An exemplary model for study. And one of the keys to its stability, as in the case of an army, is its structure of ironclad hierarchy. (Of course, its mission and values explain part of its success: there is a certain "competitive edge" to offering a meaningful answer to humankind's greatest fear, death). Down through history companies, inspired by one institution or another, have operated on the principle of hierarchy. In a hierarchical structure, power is perfectly defined and flows down from top to bottom. And as a model it has had its success...until now, at least: the drop in the number of people choosing careers in the church and the military in recent years may be a sign of the times.[12]

> In any organized group of mammals, there is always a struggle for social dominance.
> Desmond Morris, anthropologist and
> author of *The Human Zoo*

We need a certain concentration of power to live as a society! Although for rebel minds this may sound like intellectual rubbish, biological and anthropological research shows it to be true. Monkeys, wolves, and elephants all live in groups under the authority of a dominant member that is also the strongest. In the case of animals there is a symbiotic relationship: you protect me, I obey you. And if I don't like your rules, I can start my own pack with others who are willing to obey me.

The Aztecs, the Mayans, and the Incas, all of whom were sedentary, had clearly defined, well-structured hierarchies. The same is true of nomadic peoples. In the Ona tribe of Tierra del Fuego, the elders and shamans stood at the head of the social structure.[13] Thus it would seem that we need a certain concentration of power in order to live together. Other questions are what type of power, to what end and what means of opposition you have without getting your head chopped off. The Inquisition, a parking fine, or a bite from the dominant member of the pride are all examples of methods used to preserve the stability of the hierarchy. And the power granted through a democratic system is not the same as power obtained otherwise. According to Seligman,[14] democracy produces more happiness than any other political system. Having a say in who governs us presents a whole range of wonderful benefits.

...With Participation...

> It doesn't make sense to hire smart people and then tell them what to do; we hire smart people so they can tell us what to do.
>
> Steve Jobs, president of Apple

Ricardo Semler is the majority shareholder in Semco, a Brazilian shipbuilder, and he is a groundbreaking businessman. When he took over the reins of the family firm in 1982, the company had a turnover of 4 million dollars and ninety employees. By 2003, turnover had risen to 212 million and Semco was employing 3,000 people. Such exponential growth can be traced to Semler's highly innovative practices in employee management. In the early nineties, competition from Asia nearly drove the rest of the world's shipbuilding industry out of business. Semler hit back with a series of radical reforms. He imposed salary cuts, up to 40 percent for management. To compensate, he gave his employees the right to choose their hours and to decide how they wanted to be paid. Semco now offers eleven different pay schemes, from fixed salaries plus bonuses to share options that can be combined in different ways.[15] The employees assess the managers and exercise what Semler calls truly democratic management.[16] The result? In addition to overcoming the crisis and turning the company into a world leader, Ricardo Semler has received a great deal of recognition. The Wall Street Journal named him Latin American businessman of the year in 1990, the World Economic Forum named him one of its Global Leaders of Tomorrow in 1994 and in the same year *Time* featured him among its Global 100 young leaders.

What do Semco and Mondragón have in common? At first glance, not a lot. Both, however, are examples of power based on participation. Both have a formal distribution of power (of course!), but in both cases that distribution is for the benefit of the employees and of the company as a whole (an exception?). As Jesús Catania, president of Mondragón, says:[17]

> Our system is participative, not anarchic.

...And No Unwanted Backsides

Distribution of power ≠ traditional hierarchy. The traditional hierarchy is on the way out. At IBM it used to be twenty-seven steps down the hierarchy from top management to the person who made the photocopies. Now that number is seven.[18] Competition has forced the fat cats to go on slimming diet (with the help of technology). When consumers were less sophisticated (when we had no choice) strategies were designed at the main headquarters and the branch offices were limited to putting them into practice. And it worked well. These were *octopus organizations*, with a big head and a mass of tentacles. In the words of Jack Welch, the celebrated General Electric CEO until 2001:[19]

> Hierarchy is an organization with its face towards the CEO and its ass towards the customer.

To avoid unwanted backsides, companies switched from the octopus to the network model. More responsibilities were delegated to the organizational nodes, which were granted decision-making powers – even at the upper echelons of company management! But you needn't take the cooperative road or go to the extremes of a Semler. The goal is to have power at the service of the company's interests, not of the personal interests of a powerful few.

> Each loves his brief moment of authority.
>
> William Shakespeare (1564–1616)

A delicate matter? Undoubtedly so, but this is not political issue. It is a matter of pure economics. Power at the service of personal interests = Loss of potential profits. And such a debilitating formula has more than one known cure. Mondragón applies its participative principles, even in the corporations which it owns (40–50 percent of the Basque firm's employees are not cooperative members). At the international express shipper UPS, most of the shares in the company are owned by management, many of whom started out delivering packages or working an entry-level desk job.[20]At Visa International decision-making is participative.[21] At the DuPont Ibérica plants in Asturias, Spain, the workers from each section elect their own boss. These plants are among DuPont's most productive and most profitable. And some companies try to optimize performance by implementing self-management on the production line, with no interference from above.[22] Power is coming to the people. Good thing, too! And we never tire of saying it: the point is M-O-N-E-Y.

Let's sum up: companies and organizations need a formal distribution of power. But the key is whether it is participative (the more participative, the less fear it provokes) and whose interests it serves. Power can be at the service of those who have traditionally held it or at the service of the company. And it can either drive us to the precipice of fear or raise us up on the shoulders of giants and unleash the potential of our human resources. But proceed with caution: we are talking about something that can be a greater obsession than sex. Successful intervention in the power structure entails choosing the right leaders and incorporating systems that ensure that the new model will work. The forbidden fruit of power can be too tempting, and we are all potential Adams and Eves.

> If I have seen a little further it is by standing on the shoulders of giants.
>
> Isaac Newton (1643–1727)

COURAGEOUS LEADERS WANTED

Challenge: Courageous leaders who face their own fears

Courage in the Face of Dark Territories

> Whenever you see a successful business, someone once made a courageous decision.
>
> Peter Drucker, writer and
> corporate management guru

Commitment: the Holy Grail companies hunger after. Employees committed to moving mountains and capturing customers. And commitment is born not in the brain, but in enthusiasm. As Lou Gerstner, president of The Big Blue, said: "I fell in love with IBM." Where there is passion, there is commitment, and workers put their all into the company. We seek meaning, not just a salary. "People want to be involved in doing things well and to be seen as human beings," says Ken Blanchard, author of *The One Minute Manager*. And we want to make a contribution that is bigger than we are. We want to be important! And companies strive to put that into a catchy phrase: *Change the world*, Cisco Systems says, or *To boldly go where no one has gone before*, as Vivendi CEO Jean-Marie Messier once said. The mission is the destination, but the road there is traveled day by day. And leaders are the guides on that journey.

If we want commitment, we need leaders who will inspire enthusiasm rather than transmit their fears to their workers (Table 4.2). Do we ever fall in love with someone we are frightened of? Not often. The winds of change are sweeping away the old models and companies are now looking for leaders

Table 4.2 Manager or leader?

Talent-, Change-, and Innovation-oriented leader	Fear-oriented leader
You work with the boss	You work for the boss
Seeks commitment	Seeks loyalty/submission
Here you are paid to think and make decisions	*Here you are not paid to think*
Sees workers as a company asset	Sees workers as a personal asset
Lets people do their jobs	Controls people in their jobs
Treats the person as an individual	Treats the person as a resource
Sees opportunity in work environment	Sees threat in work environment
Generates trust and self-awareness	Generates insecurity and uncertainty
Gets the best out of a person	Blocks the potential of a person
Communicates course and destination	Communicates nothing
Coherence and consistency	Lack of coherence and consistency
Assumes ultimate responsibility for mistakes.	Blames team for mistakes.
Medals are for the team.	Medals are for the boss.

Source: Luis Carlos Collazos and the author.

who can unleash the energy in their workers, who offer them freedom, rather than straitjacketing them with restrictions and procedures as outdated as the iron chastity belt.

Pretty words are fine, but reality is something else all together. Being a boss is not easy. Besides the title, the car, and the office, it also means being wired to a loudspeaker that broadcasts the fears you carry within. If a manager dreads failure, he may pass that on to his workers in the form of excessive demands for perfection. If, for instance, he is reticent to go home to his family (or to his solitude, which often amounts to the same thing), he may manifest that by staying on at the office until all hours of the night. And his workers will have to follow suit.

And what is the challenge of the leader? To be courageous. Not only to have the courage to explore virgin territories, as entrepreneurs, innovators, or adventurers do, but also to dare to enter a territory even more dark and perilous: that of one's own fears. You have to unlock the door of your own potential before you can do the same for others. We must insist on this point: this is a question of money (and of happiness).

> When talent and human spirit are freed, we see that there are no limits other than those we create for ourselves.
> Santiago Álvarez de Mon, professor at IESE

Leaving People to Their Work

> The people in the trenches are the ones in the best position to make critical decisions. It's up to leaders to give those people the freedom and the resources that they need to make those decisions.
> Martin Sorrell, CEO of the
> communications services firm WPP Group

Knows	Knows how to do	Does	Makes do	Lets do
Theorist	Technician	Worker	Boss	**NoFear Leader**

Figure 4.3 From theorist to the leader

The **NoFear** leader faces a daunting personal challenge: to loosen the reins on his workers, to let them do their job (see Figure 4.3). Managers are not there to watch over or to be smarter than the rest, but to point their workers in the right direction and to give them wings (as Red Bull proclaims). Ridderstråle and Nordström put it as follows: "Gone are the days when it was assumed that the leader was a cross between John Wayne and Albert Einstein."[23] True, letting go can be a harrowing experience. "I don't exercise enough control. What is my function?" some will wonder. The control-freak boss (in the workplace, marriage, or family) destroys talent and seeks submission/obedience (yes I know it sounds funny) not commitment.

> Freedom without commitment is sterile.
> Javier Fernández Aguado and José Aguilar,
> academics and writers on leadership

Commitment is born of the freedom enjoyed by both parties (company and employee, husband and wife, fan and team), and entails an implicit mutual agreement: "I'll stick by you as long as you are valuable to me." It hardly matters what is valuable (for some it is money, professional development, or the project; for others, love, sex, or a big house). In this dance everyone moves to the same music in their own way (Table 4.3). One of the salient features of our old friend the Internet boom was that workers had the freedom, or

Table 4.3   Submission or commitment

	Commitment	Submission
Company–employee relationship	Equal standing	Unequal standing
Seeks	To achieve a goal	To avoid punishment
Founded on	Freedom	Fear
Requires	Individual initiative	Obedience

Source: The author.

power, to demand commitment, and companies had to reinvent themselves in order to make it. Submission (often confused with "loyalty") is, on the other hand, alienating, and its presence indicates a serious imbalance. Expressions like *you're either with me or against me*, or *I won't hear a bad word about it* reflect a deep-seated fear of losing control, and the belief that one should *work in the company for the boss* rather than *with the boss for the company*.[24]

> To me the worst thing seems to be a school principally to work with methods of fear, force and artificial authority. Such treatment destroys the sound sentiments, the sincerity and the self-confidence of pupils and produces a subservient subject.
>
> Albert Einstein (1879–1955)

In short, control and fear mean short-circuits in the brain. If what you want is obedient, somewhat "short-circuited" people, control is a good strategy. If you are looking for commitment, take a look at how far your urge to control has got you.

Very insecure person + job with authority = Fearmonger

Management by Exception

> If you don't understand that you work for your mis-
> labeled "subordinates,"then you know nothing of leader-
> ship. You know only tyranny.
>
> Dee Hock, Founder and CEO Emeritus,
> Visa International

The financial director of the national subsidiary of a multinational consulting firm had the policy of not allowing his
employees access to the Internet because *they might devote
their time to things other than their work!* And as happens with
all things forbidden, the Internet became a status symbol:
only the trustworthy few at the top had access. The others
went around begging for printouts of web pages. One day,
the head of IT (fancying himself an Interpol agent) discovered that someone had accessed a department store website
during working hours. A serious crime and wonderful news
for the financial director; all that was missing was the town
crier posted outside his office to proclaim just how right
he had been. Although such peccadilloes were not common practice, they became the primary justification for his
management style.

Control-freaks share a curious trait: "They manage according to the exception," as Tomás Pereda, director of Human
Resources at Hertz, says. They seize upon anecdotal inci-
dents to justify sometimes absurd but always costly measures. All of us have our dark side: nothing new in that, it
is part of our nature. If a leader loosens his grip and finds
that someone has taken advantage of the circumstances,
should he take that exception as evidence that everybody
does the same? Every family, every company has its black

sheep. And it is strange how some managers invest more time in them than in the rest of the flock. What shame for the white sheep!

Cosa Nostra

> In this company there are three golden rules: keep the people on a leash as tight as a violin string about to break; maximum dedication, putting everything into your work; and don't trust anybody, not even me...
>
> Executive from a well-known multinational with over 4,000 workers

Now there's a shining example of toxic fear. That was the advice given to a new manager on his first day of work. An extreme case, no doubt. What sort of people management, what sort of culture existed in that company? But the means of control can be more subtle and they come in all shapes and colors. Does it make sense to have employees punch a clock? Maybe it does if they are paid by the hour. If not, does it help much? If yes is the answer, perhaps the company has not done a very good job of finding responsible employees.

The CEO of a multinational with over seven million customers would walk around at the end of the workday to see who stayed longer, "generously" donating their time to the company. Paradoxes of the business world: this company has won several awards for it practices to promote a balanced personal-working life.

In a family firm with over 300 workers it was expected of department heads to join the owners for a drink after work on Friday. Extra "points" were awarded if the employee's wife came along too. This is a prime example of a practice that intrudes on a worker's private life, and a form of control in the purest Cosa Nostra style.

When Talent Is Scary

Now here's an organizational Molotov cocktail for you: a worker with talent and an insecure, control-freak boss (the same situation occurs among peers). When this sort of boss hires someone, he tends to pick someone who is not going to show him up. Of course, he will come up with a thousand and one reasons for why he rejected the best candidate, and he might even convince someone. But the real motive is simple: the fear that lurks behind these sorts of unfortunate choices, choices which eventually hit the company where it hurts most: in its profits. Perhaps we might come up with a good indicator of self-confidence: depending on whom you surround yourself with, we can tell how much trust you have in yourself.

In addition, if you find yourself playing the smart employee to the insecure, control-freak boss, you have several options: you can dress up your talent to avoid frightening the boss (massaging his ego or bald-faced flattery are two common methods); stoically hold out until your boss's boss wields the axe, the outcome of which is never a sure bet; or simply hand in your resignation. The latter is the most usual way out, when it is not the boss who makes the first move and suggests relocation to the Arctic to open an air-conditioner dealership.

In short, *nolentibus dantur*, as it says in the classics. Or as Javier Fernández Aguado and José Aguilar put it: only those people with no special interest in holding them should be promoted to positions of authority.[25] Do we apply this maxim in our companies?

Abandoning Control ...

> The life it is not a problem to solve but a mystery to experience.
>
> Luis Racionero, writer

We can change ... if we want to. No one is born a leader and everyone who takes a job in management has their own fears. When a "born control-freak" recognizes his strong points and accepts his fears, he can overcome the strongest fear of losing control. But he will need a helping hand, and here is where the crucial – and we must insist once again, profitable – support of the organization comes in.

Let us be brave and look our fears in the eye (we will return to this idea in the next chapter). Worry not if you discover some unpleasant creature within, no one is perfect. When you look your own demons in the eye, you realize that they are not so ugly after all. And when you explore your own dark side, you can help others to break their own chains and develop their own potential. *Know thyself* goes the classic maxim. We might paraphrase it as: *Know thy fears.* How much training do companies give their leaders in how to overcome their fears and explore human nature? After all the training in finance, production, and public-speaking, where is the training in what makes people tick? Once again: it's all about money, money, money ... and happiness.

Good leaders all share a common trait: deep, deep insight. They have *deep* insight into people, *deep* insight into their weak points and strong points – and a *deep* insight into how to inspire lots of trust. And, in following them, their employees make a rational, as well as emotional, decision.

Perhaps the true seat of intelligence is the heart rather than reason. An intelligent heart and sensitive reasoning make an unbeatable pair.

Santiago Álvarez de Mon, IESE professor and author of *La Lógica del Corazón*

...*With a Little Help*

A good team helps you overcome your own fears.

Pedro Luis Uriarte, president of Economía, Empresa, Estrategia

There is a saying in Spain: *Al que a buen árbol se arrima, buena sombra le cobija (If you lean to a good tree you will be protected by a good shadow)*. The trust we get from our colleagues and our level of responsibility toward them is essential to overcoming our insecurities. An army officer talking about his experience in the war in Bosnia said that, rather than his survival instincts, what weighed most heavily in his decisions was his responsibility toward his comrades. If he screwed up, the rest of the group might find themselves in danger. No wonder comradeship is one of the main motivating factors for soldiers.

When he was coaching the Chicago Bulls, Phil Jackson challenged Michael Jordan by telling him that he would be judged on how much better he made his teammates rather than on his individual performance. Jordan is considered one of the best players in the history of basketball and the architect of the Bulls' string of championship seasons. Having responsibility for the team helps a person to make decisions that he would otherwise avoid, according to Pedro Luis Uriarte. When an executive trusts his colleagues and knows that if he stumbles they will be there to cushion the fall, he can take risks. One of the keys to being a leader, then, is to stuff the cushion with more feathers, rather than building a bed of nails.

SYSTEMS FOR TUNING IN TO NOFEAR

Challenge: How to control power and promote NoFear[26]

Balancing Power

I disagree with my boss's assessment of me. I'm going to take my complaint to his boss. Suicidal tendency? Not for the employees of Hewlett Packard. The company once made a big deal of its open-door policy. If you disagreed with an important decision taken by our boss, you could file a complaint with his immediate superior and all three parties would meet to discuss their views. No one likes it when someone goes to their boss to criticize their performance, but that was part of the essence of Hewlett Packard (at least until the merger with Compaq and subsequent downsizing). If someone wanted to move to another department, they only needed to give a few months' notice, and their immediate superior had no choice in the matter. They were exercising a basic right:

> Employees are not the property of management. They are a company asset.

At the European telecommunications company Vodafone, it is the human resources departments that do the promotion planning. At the Spanish banking group BBV, promotions at the upper levels of management were agreed according to the following equation for sharing votes: 20 percent current immediate superior, 40 percent managing director, and 40 percent future superiors. Both of these are

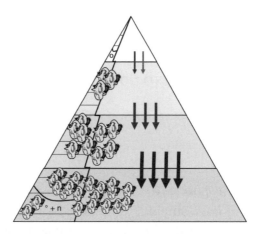

Figure 4.4 Avalanche sliding down the pyramid
Source: Tomás Pereda.

examples of systems for organizing and balancing power within companies.

No company is perfect and, no matter hard they try, sometimes a person in a position of power – acting in their own interests and against those of the company – will take a bite out of the apple of power. There is also the *avalanche effect* (Figure 4.4). But if the top management employs fear-based methods those lower down will take that as carte blanche to do the same, and they may also "enrich" the fear with input of their own. And so on, until by the time it gets to the lowest levels the fear has become an avalanche. Hence the importance of detecting fears at the source and looking for other ways to manage your people.

Snakes in Suits

> When I call a manager into my office my goal is to make him think I am going to sack him.
>
> CEO of a well-known multinational

Snakes in suits is what Robert Hare, professor emeritus of Psychology at the University of British Columbia and an authority on psychopathy, calls psychopaths who run companies.[27] Psychopath is a scary term. It conjures up images of serial killers and Norman Bates in *Psycho*. But real killers account only for 1 percent of all the psychopaths who walk this earth. So how do you spot a psychopath in a suit? What most sets them apart from others is their absolute lack of sensitivity toward the feelings of others.

When a psychopath processes information the emotional part of the brain is not activated. In other words, they are immune to the suffering of others. This is not a disease with a cure; rather it is a personality disorder which also helps psychopaths to excel in a competitive environment. As Hare says, "It is easy to find psychopaths in the highest levels of business, politics or religion." Psychopaths are highly intelligent, they have an extraordinary capacity as orators and they thrive on power – which they will pursue at any price! And, since they have no feelings for anyone else, they will stop at nothing to get what they want. And their impact on society is greater than we think. Hare estimates that 1 percent of the world population are psychopaths (of varying types and degrees, of course)[28] and that their actions affect 10 percent of the population. Guess where they are found.

A boss with psychopathic traits? If fear enables him to attain his goals, he will use it without the slightest concern for how it might affect others. All he sees is his goal. But there is a challenge.

Beware of Attila

A psychopathic boss has the same effect as Attila the Hun: wherever he has been the grass no longer grows... and nor does talent. The price is very high. Goals will be attained, without doubt, but at the cost of damages that are often impossible to repair. Our old friend collateral damage! The challenge is twofold for a company that wants to avoid having to pay those costs: on the one hand, to implement systems that encourage people to speak out against this type of behavior (so long as the boss in question is not the owner or CEO, in which case the best thing to do is simply resign) and, on the other, to get rid of such people. The first is not easy. People who are afraid of not surviving, in other words, of losing their job, will think before committing suicide in an act so heroic. You can help them overcome such fears by offering some means such as channels for making anonymous complaints. Then you of course must act accordingly; no one makes a complaint for it to end up gathering dust in a drawer somewhere (or in the bin). As for the second challenge, it must be said that sooner the decision is taken the better! And after doing so, take the time to have a good long, in-depth look at your hiring procedures.

General Electric assesses employee performance in two ways: according to how productive they are and according to how well they adapt to the company values. And they are real sticklers about the latter point. Someone may excel in productivity, but, although their conduct may be far from psychopathic, if they do not make the grade in terms of values they will be "invited" to try their luck with another company. Accordingly, General Electric sacked the managing director of one its newly acquired subsidiaries when they discovered that he subjected his female employees to systematic psychological harassment. Naturally, the employees had reported his behavior to the previous parent company, but the complaint had been "duly" filed in the bin. General Electric, however, took a hand in the matter and, despite the executive's extraordinary productivity, decided to sack him. Part of General Electric's success may well reside in how seriously it actually takes its own values, and, as in this example, not using one performance indicator to justify behavior that is damaging to the company's long-term interests.

> Remember that you have necessary, but unjustifiable, power over other people's lives. They did not elect you their manager, and so you need to be as fair and careful as you can in handling their lives.
>
> James Hoopes, author of *False Prophets*

Seeking Pelés and Ronaldinhos

Question: Is a team's performance less, equal to, or greater than the sum of its parts? The German psychologist Ringelman discovered the answer: less. He based his findings on a study he did of men pulling on a rope. According to the laws of physics, if four people pull on a rope they apply four times the force of a single person. However, Ringelman found that the true force was two and half times. And if there are eight men pulling, the ratio dropped to less than four times the individual force. Since physics is never wrong (at least in this game), it would seem that the key to the problem must lie elsewhere: motivation. Part of the combined efforts of large teams vanish, "as if by magic," due to what is known as the *group support system*.[29] When we join in a team effort, we may think: "The others aren't pulling their weight, why should I?" Or: "Why should I work harder for the same pay as everyone else?" To neutralize the Ringelman Effect we prescribe a drug called individual responsibility. Organizations must come up with schemes to recognize the work of the individual and reward those who do more for the company ... even if it is just pulling on a rope.

> You don't build your character by doing what everybody else is doing.
>
> Carlos Ghosn, CEO of Nissan

In order to encourage his employees to make decisions and incur risks, in his first year at the helm of Eli Lilly, Randall Tobias introduced rewards for failure. Quite a feat. What kind of employee does your organization reward, ones who take the initiative even at the risk of making a mistake, or the *archconservatives* (exactly the profile of many power-worshippers)? If the company rewards mediocrity, it will have mediocre employees. If it is looking for top-rank players, set the bar at the level of a Di Stefano, Pelé, or Ronaldinho and ensure that mediocre managers do not stand in their way. If you want to eliminate fear, reward employees who show talent, innovators that take decisions ... even at that risk of getting it wrong. And if you have to get rid of someone, do it nicely.

> Objectivity in a company's approval systems helps to isolate the effects of fear.
>
> Ángel Córdoba, vice managing director of Caja Madrid

Sweetening the Bitter Pill: Sackings

Five o'clock Friday afternoon and a sales executive is about to knock off for the weekend when his phone rings. "Come up to my office," the boss says at the other end of the line. So the sales exec, caught entirely off-guard by the timing of the call and the curt tone, rushes upstairs. When he gets there the boss hands him a letter informing him that he is dismissed effective immediately and that he is not to return on Monday. By this hour, all of his colleagues have gone home. He cannot go back to his desk and email them his farewells because the boss has had his Internet connection cut. His colleagues will only find out when he does not show up for work next week – the perfect way to spread fear among your workers! First because perhaps the dismissed did not see it coming (a communication breakdown along the way?), and second because his colleagues will understand that, should their turn ever come, they will get the same treatment.

Top management and human resources departments have the challenge to oversee sacking procedures. Sacking is a bitter pill to swallow, but the techniques used in the case above are not only offensive to the person who is dismissed but also to everyone else in the company. We have taken just one of hundreds of examples of how not to do it: when a security guard is waiting at the door of the boss's office to escort the person out of the building (as if the sacked employee might try to settle the matter with his fists); when an unsuspecting (former) employee is simply barred from entering the building; or when a worker comes back from a trip to find his or her things packed up in boxes, like a wayward spouse being thrown out of the nest. Many people who are sacked are potential "information thieves," and that alone should advise against treating them in this way. Likewise, we should strive to avoid "management by exception" (just because 1 percent are guilty is no justification for punishing the remaining 99 percent). The experts recommend that sacking be done on Mondays or Tuesdays so that the person can talk with their colleagues and inform properly any customers or suppliers. That is better according to Pilar Trucios, who also deals with other issues regarding such procedures.[30]

TRANSPARENCY, MISSION IMPOSSIBLE?

Challenge: Communication, communication, and communication

Hi-Tech Love

> Technology doesn't make you less stupid; it just makes you stupid faster.
>
> Thornton A. May, Manager, Toffler Associates

Forty-five million computers affected, more than 1 billion dollars in losses in the United States alone, dozens of organizations – including the Pentagon, the British Parliament, Dell Computers, and Siemens – without email... The origin: a message from a 23-year-old in the Philippines. His email, which went out on May 4, 2000, contained but one simple message: *I love you*. When opened, it unleashed one of the worst computer viruses ever. It replaced and deleted files, searched for the user's confidential information (such as passwords or addresses) and sent it back to Manila, and, more clever still, it resent the same message to all the email addresses on the infected computer. Thanks to web connectivity, the love virus spread exponentially in just a few hours, affecting organizations and individuals all over the planet. Ironically, the young Filipino had originally presented the virus as a final project for his computer studies program and the tutor had failed him on the grounds that it was impossible for such a thing to work. The creator of the virus signed his little monster: *I hate go to school*.[31] Few failing grades have taken such a toll.

The *I love you* virus shows just how cheap, quick, and effective the information and communication technologies (ICT) have made transmitting information (besides showing how the prospect of love gets millions of computer mice clicking, and how traumatic a teacher's disapproval can be). Thanks to ICT we now enjoy nearly worldwide barrier-free communication. Entire armies muster around an idea without ever seeing each other's faces, as in the case of some antiglobalization movements. Moreover, we are saturated with information. A single article in the *Herald Tribune* contains more information than what a person in the Middle Ages would have been exposed to in an entire lifetime.[32]

More Technology, More Personal Contact

Technology has also transformed organizations. IBM's Intranet posts its career opportunities and employees know what job they can apply for and how to get them. Many multinationals post their job openings, others the names of their top experts in different areas. And at Virgin, email offers direct access to the CEO's desk: Richard Branson claims that he reads all of his messages from employees. Thus technology can help to democratize companies. Power flows from whoever holds the information to whoever best knows how to use it – a process fear-based management thwarts.

> Computers are useless. They can only give answers.
> Pablo Picasso (1881–1973)

The challenge of the organization that wants to banish fear is transparency. Transparency, even with regard to news which people would rather not hear. But are we not grownups? The human mind has a proven capacity to imagine things far worse than any reality. And communication does not consist only of what comes over the Intranet or email. As they say in the Anglosphere: *high tech, high touch* (the more technology, the more personal contact). Therein lies the challenge. Webs can be the backbone of communication in a company, but they will never replace immediate contact. Even when a CEO sends out an email informing of some important matter (merger, sackings, targets) the information becomes more real when colleagues talk about it among themselves. Transparency should not only be corporate policy, but also part of top-level management. And technology, as well as immediate contact, helps to achieve that.

Cause and Effect

Thirty-five thousand years ago we invented technology. And it was then that we began to look for cause–effect relationships, according to Lewis Wolpert, professor from University College, London.[33] Presumably the first sequences were rather simple: if I strike that stone with this one, I can make fire, or mangle my thumb. Over time, the process became more sophisticated, reaching the symbolic level: if we sacrifice a calf, we will be in the gods' graces. And bit by bit, we have arrived at today with the same need to determine what the future holds. If I get a promotion, I'll be able to take over that project, or buy a bigger house. And when we cannot find any links that enable us to draw conclusions and we sail the seas of uncertainty, we feel uneasy. So it is that those who have no religious beliefs find a substitute in other types of beliefs, including superstitions. And those who are religious, no matter their faith, are happier, according to Wolpert.

Uncertainty hampers our brain. According to psychiatrists, we search for ways to control uncertainty – something to hold onto when the storm clouds appear on the horizon. But we live in times of uncertainty. The competition is unpredictable and change sweeps over us with remarkable speed. And what can a company do? It cannot control uncertainty outside its realm, but it can control it within. This is one of its greatest challenges in avoiding fear. And communication is the key.

Antidotes for Crisis

> Regard misfortune as an exercise.
>
> Seneca, philosopher (4 BC–65 AD)

Rumors of a merger. Local management gets strict orders from U.S. headquarters not to say a word about it until the terms of the buyout are settled. But, as will happen, the news has leaked out, and the evil dance of fear and uncertainty commences. Local management takes a brave decision: to communicate whatever they know at the weekly meetings. They know that the merger, which is imminent, will involve a 40 percent cut in staff and that, if they fail to tell people what is coming, no one (including management itself perhaps) will have time to find another job. Throughout the weeks of negotiations, though they have no control over the decisions being made on the other side of the Atlantic, they keep their employees up-to-date on the situation. The anxiety is palpable and such communication helps to allay fears. And quite a few families were grateful for their courage.

"In situations of crisis people are ready to hear bad news," says the executive Tomás Pereda. Why is information not shared – is it because to do so truly conflicts with the company's strategy? Or is it not shared because information is power? The challenge for **NoFear** organizations is to communicate, communicate, and communicate some more. We cannot eliminate all fears, but we can immunize ourselves against their effects. And information is a wonderful antidote, especially for damping the impact of uncertainty.

KEYS TO THE CHALLENGES FOR NOFEAR COMPANIES

- **Defensive wall**: Organizations can avoid fear-based management with the following mechanisms: Company project, power and authority, leaders, management and communication systems.

- **NoFear = Money**: Management with antifear mechanisms is aimed at improving returns.

- **Company project**: The goal is to achieve a balanced empowerment of the company's five *stakeholders* – shareholders, management, employees, customers, and society – especially employees and management.

- **Power at the service of the company**: Hierarchical power is necessary, but it must be participative and oriented toward the interests of the company, not toward those who hold it.

- **Courageous leaders**: The challenge for leaders is to set the course and let others do their jobs. To overcome the urge to overmanage, leaders must deal with their own fears.

- **NoFear Management Systems**: There are two types: those aimed at ensuring the appropriate use of power, and those which promote talent, change, and innovation.

- **Communication, communication**: the challenge for the company is to communicate, using technology, and to reduce the uncertainty caused by factors beyond its control.

5

THE CHALLENGE FOR *NOFEAR* EMPLOYEES

> People always blame their circumstances for being what
> they are. The people who get on in the world are the
> people who get up and look for the circumstances they
> want, and if they can't find them, make them.
>
> George Bernard Shaw, writer (1856–1950)

FEELING OF LOSS

John the Fearless really did exist. He was duke of Burgundy
(1371–1419), and the son of Philip the Bold (a courage-filled
family indeed). He earned his sobriquet on the battlefields
of the One Hundred Year War, during which he conquered
Paris in 1418. But rather than for his historical feats, John
the Fearless is best known as the main character in a favorite
tale by the Brothers Grimm. The story is of a young man
who sets out in search of fear because he does not know it.
But until he marries the princess, becomes the master of
the palace, and looks set to live happily ever after, he does
not feel the threat of losing what he has...and that is when
he discovers fear.

We cannot help feeling fear. We said it before: it is inher-
ent in our mammalian brain and so long as we do not suffer

some sort of brain damage – God forbid – it will remain with us. The challenge is not to fight it, but to prevent it from taking control of our lives. And, let's not kid ourselves, that is no mean feat.

The threat of fear is always subjective. Take this example. Think about a group of adolescents at the seaside. The waves are big, and some of them jump right into the water and try bodysurfing; others hang back, refusing to go in over their knees. The perception of threat, in this case a physical threat, depends on how each person interprets the dangers of the sea. Logically, here we should include other factors such as the way we were brought up, past experiences, and of course, peer pressure. In order not to be the "wimp of the pack," we can overcome our fears. This group dynamic is especially strong among adolescents.

> Self-confidence is the first secret to success.
>
> Ralph Waldo Emerson, writer (1803–1882)

What is the key to how we perceive a threat? The feeling of security or confidence in oneself and in the future. This is seen at many levels of our life: with our partners, with our friends, with our siblings ... and, of course, in the company.

On what does our self-confidence depend? On an infinite number of variables about which the psychologists do not always agree: personality, past experiences, maturity, perhaps our genes... In the case of happiness it seems that 25 to 50 percent depends on our genes.[1] So, if you come from a happy family, you have a head start over others. Moreover, fears transmitted to us by our parents and siblings may undermine our confidence. The more self-assured we are, the fewer fears we identify. In the end, our fears result either from painful situations of which we have some experience or from situations of which we have no first-hand *knowedge*. The latter case is more common and in general it is associated with greater stress.

I Grow with Fear

> That which does not kill me makes me stronger.
> Friedrich Nietzsche (1844–1900)

Daniel Gilbert, professor of psychology from Harvard University, has identified a defense mechanism in our brain that he calls the *invisible shield*.[2] What it does is make us tend to believe that our current decisions will improve our situation (what Gilbert does not say is that elderly people are immune to this effect). This system offers us all sorts of justifications. When we change jobs it might fill us with such thoughts as: *I work longer hours, but I earn more money; I don't earn as much, but I have more time to be with my children or friends*; or *I work longer hours and I earn less, but I really like the atmosphere at the new office*. Our invisible shield is very clever. Most likely, its function is to protect us from the virus of disappointment, and so horrors of failure do not seem so bad. Our invisible shield is like a salve to alleviate the pain of getting burnt and thus the demons can teach us things that would have been impossible to learn otherwise.

> A person who respects himself, that respects others, is not afraid of disappearing in relationships.
> Humberto Maturana, cognitive biologist,
> University of Chile

MEMBER OF THE AGGRESSIVE VICTIMS' CLUB

> Meaning is a shaky edifice we build out of scraps, dogmas, childhood injuries, newspaper articles, chance remarks, old films, small victories, people hated, people loved.
>
> Salman Rushdie, writer

Perhaps you find the following situation familiar: the CEO calls everyone from the company in the conference room. The climate is solemn, something which is not at all common in the company. You are wary of what is to come, and you are not the only one.

The CEO starts his speech according to the handbook: *bla-bla-bla* market is tremendously competitive, *bla-bla-bla* major changes, *bla-bla-bla* external consultants, *bla-bla-bla* new organizational structure (here starts the whispering in crescendo).

By the end of the meeting, you have probably retained but a few vague notions of the magnificent graphics subsequently presented by said consultants, ever so able in the art of PowerPoint. But certainly the basic message of the show has been etched on your brain: change, change, and more change. The CEO opened the Pandora's Box of fears – to each his or her own – which became the main topic of conversation with your colleagues by the coffee-maker or that evening with your spouse or partner.

If you see the changes as a threat (and otherwise fear would not be factor here), what avenues of action do you have when the consultants show up to "dissect" your functions? Ethology, the study of animal behavior, shows that there are four basic reactions, applicable to humans as well: aggressive defense, withdrawal, freezing, or submission (Figure 5.1).[3] The first three reactions are triggered by the

Figure 5.1 If biology ruled
Source: The author.

hypothalamus, a part of our brain that has been around for over 350 million years. Submission comes somewhat later in evolution. Of course, there are intermediate alternatives and combinations of different reactions. And, as we shall see in this chapter, we also have a much more advanced option not tied to our animal instincts: face up to our fear!

The Aggressive Victims' Club

> Effectiveness entails being in the right place at the right time and with the right intensity. It is the art of effective action in accordance with the circumstances.
>
> Sun Tzu, general and author
> of *The Art of War*, 500 AD

The best defense is a good attack, as they say, and we might add: or a *convincingly staged threat*. Which is exactly what a cat is doing when it raises its fur when frightened by a dog. And we probably did the same thing before we lost our hair in our evolution from primates to humans. We still retain a vestige of that mechanism, goose bumps, although the effect is not quite the same as when a gorilla does it. The first strategy when faced with a threat is to mount an aggressive defense, which consists lashing back at or frightening the adversary in some way, as did the armies of ancient times by beating drums as they approached the battlefield.

Aggressive defense in the company is more subtle. When we are faced with some vague but threatening change, as in the example above, it might consist of criticism: of the company, of the programme for change, of the CEO, of the consultants' ignorance of how the company works, etc., etc., etc. In short, it consists of lashing out at everything, animate and inanimate, associated with the company, especially anything that can rob you of your power. Based on this behavior tight-knit groups are formed that we might dub "aggressive victims clubs." They gather around the coffee-maker or go for lunch together and engage in endless carping about the situation, punctuated by reminders of how much better things were in the past. These are the moments for the "fix-it-all solutions"!

Playing the Fool

Take to one's heels is another idiom that we are apt to put into practice when we perceive physical danger. Which is just what an antelope or a pigeon does when they sense a predator. Rapid flight is a basic survival mechanism even in very simple organisms, such as protozoa. In such cases, biology determines behavior. In people, it can be a conscious decision to evade potential danger.

Flight is a common resource in the company. There are people who excel at evading certain responsibilities and thus having to assume any subsequent errors. When volunteers are asked to present a team's results before an audience, many will come up with a million excuses for not having to speak in public. Or when someone is given a difficult mission, he or she may try to involve as many people as possible to share the blame in the event of errors. This is the "playing the fool" technique in its purest state.

In the case of our program for change, the escape technique would be some excuse to avoid meeting with the consultants; although it is also used to avoid admitting to ourselves the possible consequences of being dispensable to the company.

Freezing up

Running away is not always recommendable when faced with a threat. If a strange noise awakens us in the middle of the night, we are likely to become petrified. Our blood goes cold and our hearing sharpens, trying to pinpoint the source (when we were little the trick was to hide under the blanket as if it were a magic shield). Many animals behave in the same way: when the turtle hides in its shell or the clever ostrich sticks its head in a hole in the ground (if I can't see them, then they can't see me). This is the freeze strategy, and it also has its manifestation in the company. Like when someone offends us, or when we are being grilled by the management committee, or when a pink slip lands on our desk, and our mind goes blank. This frozen state may last for seconds, minutes, or even days, in animals and in people if the trauma is great enough.

In our example, some rather extreme form of fear is needed in order for the person to freeze. In the meeting with the consultants, if the person felt some threat, it could cause him to lose his bearings or not know what to say. And it is not due to caution, as it might seem, this is due to the psychological block caused by fear.

Whatever You Say, Sir

Whatever you say, sir is what we might call the last strategy: submission, of which we have previously spoken. More evolved animals (more evolved than a snake or a frog, say) also use submission in their social relations, although never with a predator. When a young lion exposes its neck to a dominant male, it is expressing its approval and submission.

Similar phenomena occur in companies. Often employees will disagree with an order but submit nonetheless with barely a grumble, or even worship the boss for it. This technique achieves two things: by submitting to authority we avoid fear, and we reap the benefits of having bolstered the boss's ego. Power worship is what is known in colloquial language as *sucking up to someone, brownnosing, licking the boss's boots*, or *playing the teacher's pet....*In short, *whatever you say, sir.*

What a marvelous program. *This is just change we needed.* Precisely the sort of answers someone who employs this strategy would give to the consultants – despite sensing a threat within and not liking the CEO's big idea one bit.

All of the above are biological formulas, but we have another: the ability to face our own fear and look it in the eye.

> The most terrifying thing is to accept oneself completely.
>
> Carl Gustav Jung, psychologist and psychiatrist (1875–1961)

LOOKING FEAR IN THE EYE

Challenge: Look fear in the eye

> We can never know what we fear; to know something it
> is necessary to lose your fear of it, and if you are afraid of
> yourself, you shall never know yourself.
> Miguel de Unamuno, writer (1864–1936)

We Want Meaning

World War II was one of the most horrifying episodes
in human history, and the setting for a demonstration
of one of the most interesting findings in the history of
thought: the human need to find meaning in life. Viktor
Frankl[4] was a Jewish psychiatrist who was imprisoned for
three years in concentration camps during the war. He
observed that those who managed to survive that trag-
edy were not the strongest, not the cleverest, but those
who had an ultimate reason for living: to see a spouse or
children again, to help their fellow prisoners, to write a
book, or make a journey that they had long dreamt of. In
short, a mission more important than themselves which
gave them the strength to overcome their fears, even
those of the worst horrors of Auschwitz. And it seems that
that strength has roots in the internal workings of our
immunological system, designed to defend us from illness and death.

Frankl sums up the search for the meaning of life as
follows:

> It does not really matter what we expect from life, but rather
> what life expects from us. We need to stop asking about the
> meaning of life, and instead to think of ourselves as those who
> are being questioned by life – daily and hourly.

The need to find meaning in what we do presents a major challenge for companies. The book *Gestión del Talento*[5] lists three types of factors on which our commitment depends: external factors (money, status), internal factors (training, development), and transcendental factors (mission and values). It is precisely this last source of motivation that moves mountains, passions, or talent. When someone is bound to their mission – sometimes called will – they are capable of giving their all for the project. And that is what our own experience tells us. We are stronger when we believe in what we are doing and when we give it a larger meaning: to write as a contribution to something is not the same as doing so for vanity, as Jordi Nadal says. Nor is giving a speech in order to do your part the same as doing it just to avoid bigger problems. The search for meaning transforms our way of working and it immunizes us against fear (albeit only partially).

Seligman had a student who was frustrated with her job. She worked in a supermarket bagging groceries. A rather dull way to earn a living, without doubt. But Seligman helped her to see it in a different light. First, he identified her strong points as a person. In this case, she excelled at social interaction. And second, he applied it to her job. He had her set herself the goal of making the check-out process a positive experience and the high-point of each customer's day. She discovered a motivation and thus found satisfaction in her job. And this might seem like an irrelevant example, given the simplicity of the job or the obviousness of the solution (the opinion of the supermarket's least sociable customers notwithstanding), but until we invent machines to bag groceries we must remember that people are people, and people need to find meaning in what they do. ... And what meaning have you found?

> If you have your own why in life, almost any how will do.
> Friedrich Nietzsche (1844–1900)

And what is more: if you do not have a why, you will fall prey to fear. When you have a mission that is larger than yourself, you can draw strength from your weaknesses, as they say. And here's nobody's secret: we are capable of turning our fears into reality! That is exactly what happened to the Austrian composer Arnold Schönberg (1874–1951). He had absolute dread of the number thirteen. He avoided doing important things on any thirteenth of the month. In the end, he died on a Friday the 13th, at 13 minutes to midnight. Clairvoyance or self-fulfilling prophecy? When someone becomes obsessed with an idea, whether it is good or bad, they will eventually make it a reality.

The way to avoid fear is not by attacking it. That would be absurd, because it would mean attacking ourselves and the only thing we would achieve would be to strengthen it. The alternative is hitching ourselves to a mission that transcends each of us. As Frankl says: "What man actually needs is not a tensionless state but rather the striving and struggling for some goal worthy of him." The fear is out there, but if we commit ourselves wholeheartedly to our ultimate goals we immunize ourselves against part of its effects.

And So?

> And not only does fear displace love; it also displaces intelligence, goodness, all thought of beauty and truth,

and all that remains is quiet desperation; and in the end, fear comes to displace the humanity in man himself.

Aldous Huxley, writer (1894–1963)

One of the techniques for overcoming the fear of flying is to imagine the plane crash that you are so terrified of. Starting a few weeks before a flight, you spend a few minutes every day imagining the hypothetical events as they unfold: the fire fighters rushing onto the scene, the television crew … the whole drama in all its gory details. And so on day after day, picturing the same plane, the same fire fighters, the same television reporter in his same old tie. Then when you finally get on the plane, you are so tired of imagining the same scenes over and over again that your mind simply forgets your fear and turns to other thoughts. In some cases this technique is very effective. When we "dissect" our fears (using common sense to define them), we find that they are not so terrible. Let's not forget that we are our own worst enemy. And at imagining ambiguous and terrible situations we are great experts.

William Golding, Nobel Prize winner for Literature in 1983, wrote *The Lord of the Flies*, the classic tale of a group of schoolboys and their struggle to survive on an island after their plane crashes. In order to gain power over the group, one of the leaders invents a fear: a monster that could devour them. This is an example of an ambiguous fear, hardly real but quite effective. By this device, he frightens the other boys and strengthens his hold over them.

> I must not fear. Fear is the mind-killer. Fear is the little-death that brings total obliteration. I will face my fear. I will permit it to pass over me and through me. And when it has gone past I will turn the inner eye to see its path.

Where the fear has gone there will be nothing. Only I will remain.

Frank Herbert, *Dune* (1965)

Panic in the family. One of the breadwinners, father or mother, has lost their job. Conversation round the dinner table is filled with fears: mortgage, school fees, holidays, what will our friends think. ... After a time (depending on the person's employability, the market, and contacts), he or she embarks on a new professional life. There is a nearly universal maxim: *Everyone gets by*. It may be with less money or a lower status, but you are sure to get back on your feet again. In difficult situations, some Eastern cultures take a different view: *So what*? So what if I lose my status? Does it change who I am? No, but it does affect what you have. When you are committed to your mission (and to yourself), you can face fear without fear.

> If I am what I have and if I lose what I have who then am I? Nobody but a defeated, deflated, pathetic testimony to a wrong way of living.
>
> Erich Fromm, philosopher (1900–1980)

To Have or To Be?

> Individuals want to be happy, and societies want individuals to consume.
>
> Daniel Gilbert, psychology professor,
Harvard University

To have or to be? That is the title of a book by Erich Fromm, one of the fathers of contemporary humanistic philosophy – and it is the dichotomy we face in defining our mission. To have has become our identity. And it seems a bit of a paradox to seek individuality in a mass-produced BMW, even if it does cost 60,000 euros. In the identity-consumption tandem, there are the winners (companies and their employees) and there are the losers (people who are besieged by fears of losing what they have). When we play this game, change – in our job, the arrival of a competitor, or early retirement – is perceived as a threat. And perhaps we are not so aware of the fact that when our ambition is based on what we are, change may produce certain unease, but rarely fear. Pilar Gómez Acebo sums it as follows: "Those who work to be are born winners." But the challenge is not so easy.

In a survey done some years ago in France, 89 percent of those questioned agreed that man needs something to live for.[6] Viktor Frankl says that the neurosis of our society is our existential void. And our response is to fill that void with superficial things: material goods, professional status. ... In short, everything we subsequently become afraid of losing. It is hardly surprising that the number of people who undergo plastic surgery has grown exponentially in recent years; the loss of the physical beauty has become one of the great obsessions of our day. We now associate self-fulfillment with the personal success of having, rather than that of being. And here's the big question: Are companies interested in people motivated by being or by having? When executives say they want salespeople with the best homes and the best cars, exactly what are they looking for? The pursuit of possessions makes us more vulnerable to fear and, without doubt, to manipulation of our void. If the company wants talent, its challenge is to make its employees work toward an ultimate goal that is greater than just having. Cars are wonderful, of course, but we also work for something more transcendental, something which gives us the meaning obtained from having made a contribution.

> Traveller, there is no way, only the wake in the sea.
> Antonio Machado, poet (1875–1939)

One last suggestion: face your fear, think about its exact cause and what the alternative solutions might be. Avoid ambiguous fears, recognize the monster from *The Lord of the Flies* for what it is: a harmless if scary corpse. By doing so you will be able to stand back from and get a perspective on your fears. And if, following the advice of Viktor Frankl, you can laugh at your fears, all the better. A sense of humor is, in addition to being an evident sign of maturity, another excellent therapy for fear. Humor distances us from our emotions and helps us to put them in perspective. If you look back and examine all the fears you have overcome in the past (of failing an exam, of not being accepted by your peers, ... and a long etcetera), you will see that they were not so terrible as they seemed at the time. We are much bigger than our fears!

It is not too late to free yourself of your fears. Do you accept the challenge?

> Today is most beautiful day in our life, dear Sancho;
> the greatest obstacles, our own hesitations;
> our strongest enemy, the fear of the mighty and of ourselves;
> the easiest thing, to err;
> the most destructive, lies and selfishness;
> the worst defeat, dismay;
> the most dangerous defects, pride and spite;
> the most welcome sensations, good conscience,
> the effort to be better
> without being perfect, and above all, the will to do good
> and fight injustice wherever it may be found
> Ascribed to Miguel de Cervantes, author of *Don Quixote*

KEYS TO THE CHALLENGES FACING NOFEAR PROFESSIONALS:

- **Feeling of loss**: Fear arises from the threat of losing what we have. And that threat depends on how secure and confident we feel about ourselves.

- **Invisible shield**: Helps us to deal with fear by showing us that today's decisions always lead to new situations that are an improvement on the past.

- **Biological strategies against fear**: When frightened, we tend to react with aggressive defense, freezing, withdrawal, or submission.

- **NoFear Challenge**: Overcoming fear not only entails confronting it, but also finding strength in a mission that transcends yourself.

- **Define, please**: Ambiguous fears haunt us. Using common sense, we must define them: only then can we look them in the eye and look for solutions. Moreover, in the end we will get by.

- **To have or to be?** Base your mission and self-esteem on being, not on having: that is a sure way of dealing with fear. That and a sense of humor to distance yourself from fear.

NOTES

1 FEAR UNDER THE MICROSCOPE

1. Martin, R. (1996): *Diccionario de la mitología griega y romana*. Madrid: Espasa de Bolsillo.
2. The New Oxford Dictionary of English. Oxford University Press, 2003.
3. Walk, R.D. and Gibson, E.J. (1961): "A Comparative and Analytical Study of Visual Depth Perception," *Psychological Monographs*, 75, 519.
4. Marks, I (1991): *Miedos, fobias y rituales: Los mecanismos de la ansiedad*. Barcelona: Martínez Roca.
5. Thanks to Tomás Pereda for his input on this point.
6. Gallagher, M. (2004): *Handbook of Psychology*. Book online.
7. Daniel Goleman and Mario Alonso Puig describe the relationship between the brain and emotions. Goleman, D. (1996): *Inteligencia emocional*. Barcelona: Kairós. Alonso Puig, Mario (2004): *Madera de Líder. Barcelona*: Empresa Activa.
8. Paul McLean, director of Laboratory for Brain Evolution and Behavior in California, proposes that we have three superimposed neuronal systems resulting from our evolutionary process: reptilian brain, limbic brain, and rational brain or neocortex. The reptilian, or encephalic stem, is the oldest and is responsible for certain patterns of aggression, our instinct to defend our territory, and basic sexual instincts. The second neuronal system, the limbic, which we share with other mammals, houses the amygdala. The neocortex is what differentiates us from all other animals. Language, creativity, and artistic thought are developed there. But the neocortex does not act like a "lone ranger," rather it works in conjunction with the rest of the brain, especially with the amygdala. And we are fortunate that it is that way. Otherwise, mothers would not feel bonds with their

children. The offspring of animals without a neocortex, such as snakes, have to hide from their mother so that they are not eaten. In this sense the relationship is positive. But it has other activities which are not so beneficial: It can short-circuit our talent, especially, when we are afraid. MacLean, P.D. (1990): *The Triune Brain in Evolution: Role in Paleocerebral Functions*. New York: Plenum Press.

9. Ledoux, J. (2002): *Synaptic Self. How Our Brains Become Who We Are*. New York: Viking.

10. Selye, H. (1975): *Tensión sin angustia*. Madrid: Guadarrama.

11. Sapolsky, R.M. (1995): *¿Por qué las cebras no tienen úlcera? La guía del estrés*. Madrid: Alianza.

12. Riftin, Jeremy: "La vida a la velocidad de la luz: ¿Estamos mejor?," http://usuarios.lycos.es/politicasnet/articulos/vidaluz.htm (accessed December 2004).

13. Ibid.

14. American Institute of Stress.

15. Corticoids in excessive doses impede the action of a type of white corpuscles, lymphocytes NK, which prevent the formation of cancerous tumors. Alonso Puig (2004).

16. Gray, A. (1971): *La psicología del miedo*, Madrid: Ediciones Guadarrama.

17. Thomas Henry Huxley. http://www.ucmp.berkeley.edu/history/thuxley.html (accessed September 2005)

18. *Business 2.0*, June 13, 2000.

19. Ekman, P., Davidson, R.J., and Friesen, W.V. (1990): "Duchenne's smile: Emotional Expression and Brain Physiology II," *Journal of Personality and Social Psychology*, 58: 342–353.

20. It seems that there is no consensus regarding basic emotions, with each author proposing his or her own theory. Reeve, J. (1994): *Motivación y emoción*. Madrid. Mc Graw-Hill.

21. Damasio, A. (1996): *El error de Descartes*. Barcelona: Crítica.

22. The theoretical foundations of traditional Chinese medicine go back more than two thousand years. It is based on the assumption that the combination of our emotions and the external factors that affect the organism, such as a change in seasons or weather, are the pathological base of illness. The tradition also holds that each person, living between heaven and earth, constitutes a miniature universe of his or her own. Illness occurs when our inner harmony is disturbed. Accordingly, in the Chinese medical tradition, fear is a manifestation of an imbalance that

affects the entire person. The important thing is the person as a whole, not the illness. "Chinese Medicine" at the website of the Government of Taiwan. http://www.gio.gov.tw (accessed November 2004).

2 FEARS À LA CARTE

1. Source: Exhibitor Relations Co., Inc.
2. McClelland, D.C. (1985): *Human Motivation*. Cambridge: Cambridge University Press.
3. Gueshe Kelsang Gyatso School.
4. Maslow, A. (1954): *Motivation and Personality*. New York: Harper.
5. Report on Youth in Spain (2000). Can be downloaded at http://www.mtas.es/injuve/biblio/estudio_injuve/estucronologico/informe2000.htm (accessed September 2005).
6. Sennett, R. (1998): *The Corrosion of Character: The Personal Consequences of Work in the New Capitalism*. New York: W.W. Norton & Company.
7. *Business Week*, October 4, 1999.
8. Asch, S.E. (1952): *Social Psychology*. Englewood Cliffs, NJ: Prentice Hall.
9. Janis, I.L. (1972): *Victims of Groupthink*. Boston: Houghton Mifflin Company.
10. Lamo de Espinosa, E.; González García, J.M., and Torres Albero, C. (1994): *La sociología del conocimiento y de la ciencia*. Madrid: Alianza.
11. McClelland (1985).
12. The Bible, Gospel of Matthew, chapter 19, verse 21–30.
13. McClelland (1985).
14. Fromm, E. (2003): *El miedo a la libertad*. Barcelona: Paidós.
15. McClelland (1985).
16. Jericó, P. (2001): *Gestión del talento, del profesional con talento al talento organizativo*. Madrid: Prentice Hall; *Financial Times*.
17. Herzberg, F., Mausner, B., and Snyderman, B.B. (1959): *The Motivation to Work*. New York: John Wiley & Sons.
18. Peters, T. (2005): *50 claves para hacer de usted una marca*. Barcelona: Gestión 2000.
19. Elffers, J. and Greene, R. (1998): *The 48 Laws of Power*. New York: Viking Press.

20. French J.R.P. and Raven, B. (1959): "The Bases of Social Power," in Cartwright, D. (ed.), *Studies in Social Power*. University of Michigan Press.
21. Peter, L. (1969): *The Peter Principle*. New York: William Morrow and Company.
22. Fernández Aguado, J. and Aguilar, J. (2004): *La soledad del directivo*. Madrid: Mind Value.
23. Sapolsky (1995).
24. Ridderstråle, J and Nordström, K.A. (2004): *Karaoke Capitalism*. Madrid: Prentice Hall.
25. Handy, C. (2001): *The Elephant and the Flea*. London: Hutchinson.
26. Ridderstråle and Nordström (2004).
27. McWhirter, J. (2004): "Arte y la ciencia de los hábitos efectivos," *Curso SCT*, Sigüenza, March.
28. Pylyshyn (1984), cited in Delclaux, Isidoro (1982): *Psicología cognitiva y procesamiento de la información*. Madrid: Ediciones Pirámides.

3 THE PRICE OF FEAR

1. Report *El negocio de lo falso*. Falsifications account for 5 to 7 percent of world trade, that is, some 500 billions euros per year.
2. *Business Week*, August 28, 2000.
3. Study *Talento Miedo y Resultados*.
4. Alonso Puig (2004).
5. Tischler, Linda (2005): "The CEO's New Clothes," *Fast Company*, 98, September.
6. Jericó (2001).
7. Martha Rogers. Expomanagement, May 11 and 12, 2005. Madrid.
8. The divorce rate in Sweden is 60 percent (Ridderstråle and Nordström, 2004) and in Mexico it is 40 percent. Cimac (2004): "Seis de cada 10 parejas se separan en México," Cimac Noticias, January 19, http://www.cimacnoticias.com/noticias/04ene/04011903.html (accessed May 2005)
9. Klein, N (2001): *No logo. El poder de las marcas*. Barcelona: Paidós.
10. *The Industry Standard*, June 19, 2000.
11. Ridderstråle and Nordström (2004).
12. *Residence*, 4, 2003.
13. Carlzon, J. (1987): *Moments of Truth*. New York: Ballinger Publishing Company.

14. The Economist (1999): *The World in 2000*. London.
15. Handy (2001).
16. Reinoso, José (2004): "China crea un gigante informático tras la compra de Lenovo paga en la mayor operación de una empresa china en el exterior," *El País*, 9, December.
17. Cambio (2005): "La nueva conquista," *Cambio*, 18–25 July.
18. Vahtera, J., Kivimäki, M., Pentti, J., Linna, A., Virtanen, M., Virtanen, P., Ferrie, J.E. (2004): *Organisational Downsizing, Sickness Absence, and Mortality: 10-Town Prospective Cohort Study, BMJ*, February 23, 2004. Downloadable at *BMJ* Online First bmj.com
19. Wyatt, W. (1991): "Reestructuring – Cure or Cosmetic Surgery?," cited in Bonache, J. (2002): "Retención y ruptura laboral" in Bonache and Cabrera (dir.) *Dirección estratégica de personas*. Madrid: Prentice Hall.
20. Bonache (2002) *op.cit.*
21. Roach, J. (2001): "Delphic Oracle's Lips May Have Been Loosened by Gas Vapors," *National Geographic News* August 14. Available online at http://news.nationalgeographic.com/news/2001/08/0814_delphioracle.html (accessed summer 2005)
22. Lorenz, C. and Leslie, N. (1992): *The Financial Times on Management*. London: Pitman Publishing.
23. "Leading in Unnerving times," *Sloan Management Review*, special issue 42 (2), December 2001.
24. *Fast Company*, August 2000.
25. El Mundo (2003): "El tiempo de fabricación de un coche, clave del ahorro para PSA," *El Mundo*, January 30.
26. http://www.slowfood.com
27. Torrecilla, José Miguel (1999): "Las estrategias operativas de las empresas," *Economía Industrial*, no. 330, VI.
28. Suárez, G. (1997): *Miedo en las Organizaciones*. Asturias Business School, Barcelona: Ediciones Juan Granica, S.A.
29. Torrecilla, José Miguel (1999): "Las estrategias operativas de las empresas," *Economía Industrial*, no. 330, VI.
30. www.nokia.com
31. Seligman, M. (2003): *La auténtica felicidad*. Barcelona: Paidós.
32. www.fortune.com
33. *Financial Times*, April 24, 2001.
34. Khermouch, Gerry, Holmes, S., and Ihlwan, Moon. (2001): "The Best Global Brands," *BusinessWeek*, August 6.

35. Hamilton, C (2004): "Carpe Diem?, The Deferred Happiness Syndrome," *The Australian Institute*. https://www.tai.org.au/file.php?file=WP57.pdf
36. Pocock, B. and Clark, J. (2004): "Downshifting in Australia: A Sea Change in the Pursuit of Happiness," *The Australia Institute*, Discussion Paper no. 50, Canberra.
37. Seligman (2003).
38. The top-selling drugs in the world are as follows: cholesterol and triglyceride reducers (30.2 billion dollars), antiulcerants (25.5), cytostatics (23.8) and antidepressants (20.3). Source: IMS Health Intelligence 360. Published in Correo Farmacéutico, June 27, 2005.
39. Doctor Elisabeth Kubler-Ross has written more than one dozen books, including *Death, A Final Stage of Growth* and *The Wheel of Life*. http://www.elisabethkublerross.com/

4   CHALLENGE FOR *NOFEAR* ORGANIZATIONS

1. Nature (2005): "The Chimpanzee Genome," *Nature*, 437 (7055).
2. Malone, T. (2004): *The Future of Work*. Boston MA: Harvard Business School Press.
3. Forcadell, F. (2005): "Democracia, cooperación y éxito. Implicaciones prácticas del caso de Mondragón," *Universia Business Review*, April.
4. www.fortune.com
5. Forcadell (2005).
6. www.enron.com, October 1998
7. Strozza, P. (2002): "La catastrófica quiebra de Enron se vio primero en Internet," *Clarín.com*, January 24.
8. www.ebay.com (accessed October 12, 2004).
9. Reich, R.B. (2000): The Future of Success. New York: Alfred A. Knopft.
10. Jericó (2001).
11. Thanks to David Aguado for his comments on this point.
12. *Economist*, April 12, 2003.
13. Aguila, Arnoldo: *Jerarquía, Propiedad y Dinero*, http://www.arnoldoaguila.com/jerarquia.html (accessed May 2005).
14. Seligman (2003).
15. Handy, C (2001): "Why Companies May be Held to Ransom by Their Employees," *European Business Forum*, 6, Summer.
16. Semler, R. (2001): *Radical*. Barcelona: Gestión 2000.
17. Cited in Forcadell (2005).

18. "Venid the numbers," *Harvard Business Review*, August 2003.
19. Ridderstråle and Nordström (2004).
20. Labich, K. (1988): "Big Changes at Big Brown," *Fortune*, January 18: 56.
21. Malone (2004).
22. Kreitner, R. and Kinicki, A. (2001): *Organizational Behavior*. New York: McGraw-Hill.
23. Ridderstråle and Nordström (2004).
24. Luis Carlos Collazos.
25. Fernández Aguado, F. and Aguilar, J. (2004): *La soledad del directivo*. Madrid: Mind Value.
26. The book *Gestión del Talento* describes NoFear systems for selecting, developing, and retaining professionals (Prentice Hall, 2001).
27. Hare, R. (2003): *Sin conciencia. El inquietante mundo de los psicópatas que nos rodean*. Barcelona: Paidós.
28. Ibid.
29. Shepperd, J.A. (1993): "Productivity Loss in Performance Groups: A Motivation Analysis," *Psychological Bulletin*, 1.
30. Trucios, P. (2001): "En España los despidos se hacen tarde y mal," *Expansión y Empleo*, June 7.
31. Alzaba, Pedro and Pastor, Enric (2000): "El virus del amor colapsa ordenadores de todo el mundo," *El Diario del Navegante*, http://www. el-mundo.es/navegante (accessed May 2005).
32. Kets de Vries, M. (2001) *The Leadership Mystique: A User's Manual for the Human Enterprise*, London: Prentice Hall.
33. Wolpert, L. (1998): *The Unnatural Nature of Science*. Boston MA: Harvard Business School Press.

5 THE CHALLENGE FOR *NOFEAR* EMPLOYEES

1. Seligman (2003).
2. Gilbert, D. (1984): *The Handbook of Social Psychology*. New York: Oxford University Press and McGraw-Hill.
3. Marks, I. (1991): *Miedos, fobias y rituales: Los mecanismos de la ansiedad*. Barcelona: Martínez Roca.
4. Frankl, Viktor (1946/2004): *El hombre en busca de sentido*. Barcelona: Herder.
5. Jericó (2001).
6. Cited in Frankl, Viktor (1946/2004).

INDEX